NORTH BY NORTHWEST

NORTH BY NORTHWEST
Ernest Lehman

faber and faber

First published in 1999
by Faber and Faber Limited
3 Queen Square London WC1N 3AU

Photoset by Parker Typesetting Service, Leicester
Printed in England by Clays Ltd, St Ives plc

North by Northwest © 1959 Turner Entertainment Co.
All rights reserved.
Printed with the consent of Turner Entertainment
Written by Ernest Lehman
Introduction © Ernest Lehman, 1999
Photographs courtesy of Ernest Lehman

Ernest Lehman is hereby identified as author of this
work in accordance with Section 77 of the
Copyright, Designs and Patents Act 1988

A CIP record for this book
is available from the British Library

ISBN 0-571-20184-9

2 4 6 8 10 9 7 5 3 1

CONTENTS

Ernest Lehman, Eva Marie Saint and Alfred Hitchcock.

INTRODUCTION

In movie theaters and on television sets around the world, it seems as though *North by Northwest* will go on for ever. Forty-some-odd years ago, it seemed to me that *writing* that film would go on for ever, too. Actually, it took me a year.

Composer Bernard Herrmann had brought Alfred Hitchcock and me together for lunch one day because Benny thought the two of us would get along rather well. We did, and after lunch, I stood happily beside Hitch watching him shoot scenes for *Rear Window* at Paramount. Soon after, he requested, through our mutual agent, that I write the screenplay for *The Wreck of the Mary Deare* at MGM, who had bought the novel for him.

I couldn't see a movie in it. I turned him down.

Hitch was furious, I was told.

Our mutual agent then talked him (and me) into having lunch at the Polo Lounge of the Beverly Hills Hotel. We had such a good time together that I agreed to do *Mary Deare*. But after three weeks of beating-around-the-bush story conferences at his Bel Air home, I arrived one morning and said, 'I have bad news for you, Hitch. I don't know how to do this picture. You'll have to get yourself another writer.'

'Don't be silly,' he said calmly. 'We get along so well. We'll do something else instead.'

'But what'll we tell MGM?' I said.

'We won't tell them,' he replied, straight-faced.

'Something else' became two months of back-and-forth ping-ponging of ideas, some of them good, but not for me. One day I said, 'All I want to do is write the Hitchcock picture to end all Hitchcock pictures.'

'And what would that be?' he enquired.

I shrugged. 'Something with wit, glamor, sophistication, suspense, many different colorful locals, a real movie movie.'

He said nothing for a while. Then he murmured wistfully, 'I always wanted to do a chase across the faces of Mount Rushmore.'

'Hey!' I exclaimed, straightening up in my chair.

Hitchcock and Lehman in the broiling sun of Bakersfield, California, discussing camera angles for the crop-duster sequence.

There followed many weeks in which we tried to figure out who was chasing whom, and why. Meanwhile, Hitch had to devote a good deal of his attention to a little something he was preparing called *Vertigo*. I alternated between phoning him and asking for more meetings, and phoning my agent and telling him to get me off this impossible project. 'You can't quit,' my agent said. 'You already quit once. Get back to work.'

Hitch was much more helpful. 'I always wanted to do a scene,' he said one day, 'where our hero is standing all alone in a wide open space and there's nobody and nothing else in sight for three hundred and sixty degrees around, as far as the eye can see . . . and then along comes a tornado. No place to run.'

'But wait a minute,' I said. 'How can the heavies manufacture a *tornado*?'

Thus was the crop-duster sequence born, acted out, shot-by-shot, by Hitch and me in the living-room of his home. I played the plane. He played the diesel truck.

I hammered out a partial outline. Hitch informed the front office what I was up to. The executives were delighted, assuming they'd get two Hitchcock pictures instead of one. Hitch went off to shoot *Vertigo*. I headed east on a much-needed research trip: the adventures of Roger Thornhill, a.k.a. George Kaplin.

First stop, New York City – the Plaza Hotel. Where to stage a kidnapping? Then to the United Nations. Where to commit murder? Then to Glen Cove, Long Island, where I persuaded a cooperative judge to put me through the experience of being arrested for drunk driving, I took the *Twentieth Century Limited* to Chicago (but never met an 'Eve'), explored the Ambassador East Hotel, covered a Chicago auction, trained to Rapid City, South Dakota, stayed at the Sheraton Johnson Hotel, hired a forest ranger on his weekend off, and started climbing one of the faces of Mount Rushmore. Halfway to the top, I looked down dizzily. 'I'm a screenwriter. What am I doing up here?' I cried. 'I could get killed!'

I clambered down, bought a Polaroid camera, and had the forest ranger photograph the entire top of the monument. It turned out there was no place up there for a scene. (Later, the US Department of National Park refused to allow Hitch to shoot at Mount Rushmore, and the United Nations said no, too. No problem.

ix

Gifted production designer Robert Boyle created the amazing Faces of the Presidents on the sound stages of MGM, and his magical sets also gave the film Vandamm's getaway house near the monument and the interior of the United Nations, as well.)

Now I had nothing left to do, no place else to go, no time left to stall, so I returned to California and started the endless task of writing a screenplay in my lonely office #206, the Thalberg Building, MGM, while Hitch finished *Vertigo* and took a desperately needed vacation in the British West Indies.

I mailed the first half of my work to him and received a cheerful, cheering four-page hand-written letter from Round Hill Hotel, Montego Bay, Jamaica. 'My dear Ernie . . . Let me say how much I enjoyed the sixty-five pages. I really thought they were excellent. And so amusingly written. You have done a fine job . . . Love, Hitch.'

Buoyed by his words and galvanized into action, I spent the next several months attacking my reluctant Underwood typewriter in fits and starts, while at the other end of the building, Hitch and his staff moved in and began preparing, sketching, casting and designing the picture we called, at one time or another, 'In a Northwesterly Direction', 'The Man in Lincoln's Nose,' and 'North by Northwest', working titles, of course, telling ourselves we'd come up with the *real* title one day (and neither Hitch nor I realized until after the movie's release that, technically, there was no such direction as NNW).

Finally, disaster struck. My Underwood had fallen silent. For two whole weeks, I couldn't think of a word to write. Cary Grant had started on salary. Hitch was busy wardrobing Eva Marie Saint, and there I was with no third act, just blank pages. I had no idea why *anybody* was headed for the vicinity of Mount Rushmore.

I picked up the phone. 'Hitch, we're in trouble.'

'I'll be right there,' he said quickly. He didn't want trouble in *his* office. I gave him the bad news. We sat staring at each other.

'We'll hire a mystery writer,' he said. 'A novelist, to come in and throw ideas at us.'

'But what'll they say upstairs?' I cried. 'I'm supposed to be the writer!'

'I'll tell them it's my fault,' he said. 'I wasn't able to help you enough.' I kept looking at Hitch and I really was listening to him as he slowly listed the names of all the famous suspense novelists of the day. But suddenly my right brain spoke up, and I heard myself saying, 'She takes a gun out of her purse and shoots him.'

Hitch's eyes widened. 'In the Polish Underground, sometimes they killed one of their own to show that *they* weren't one of them.'

'Hitch,' I said, 'they're not real. They're fake bullets.' After that, it was easy. The whole third act fell into place just like that.

These days, as always, movie-goers like to find holes in the story. I usually offer them a fleet of trucks. Only the other day, I drove through a new hole myself. Thornhill is peering through binoculars at the faces of the presidents. 'I don't like the way Teddy Roosevelt is looking at me,' he says uneasily to the Professor, seated nearby. Go see the picture again. The way his face is positioned. Teddy Roosevelt isn't looking at *anyone*.

Ernest Lehman, 1999

CREDITS

CAST

ROGER THORNHILL	Cary Grant
EVE KENDALL	Eva Marie Saint
PHILLIP VANDAMM	James Mason
CLARA THORNHILL	Jessie Royce Landis
PROFESSOR	Leo G. Carroll
LESTER TOWNSEND	Philip Ober
HANDSOME WOMAN	Josephine Hutchinson
LEONARD	Martin Landau
VALERIAN	Adam Williams
HERBERT LARRABEE	Edward Platt
LICHT	Robert Ellenstein
AUCTIONEER	Les Tremayne
DR CROSS	Philip Coolidge
CHICAGO POLICEMAN	Pat McVey
CAPTAIN JUNKET	Edward Binns
CHICAGO POLICEMAN	Ken Lynch

THE FILM-MAKERS

Produced by	Alfred Hitchcock
Directed by	Alfred Hitchcock
Screenplay by	Ernest Lehman
Music by	Bernard Herrmann
Photographed by	Robert Burks, A.S.C.
Production Designed by	Robert Boyle
Art Direction	William A. Horning and Merrill Pye
Set Decoration	Henry Grace Frank McKelvey
Special Effects	A. Arnold Gillespie and Lee LeBlanc
Titles Designed by	Saul Bass
Edited by	George Tomasini, A.C.E.
Color Consultant	Charles K. Hagedon
Recording Supervisor	Franklin Milton
Hair Styles by	Sydney Guilaroff
Make-up by	William Tuttle
Assistant Director	Robert Saunders
Associate Producer	Herbert Coleman

North by Northwest

A SERIES OF STREET SCENES

*Over them, the credits. These scenes should capture the tempo of
Madison Avenue and Fifth Avenue in the fifties. Streets swarming with
smartly dressed people. Revolving doors of sleek glass-and-steel office
buildings spewing out streams of super-charged New Yorkers, hurrying
for cabs and buses and subways and cocktail bars. Two bundle-laden
women fighting over a cab. A packed bus closing its doors in the face of
an irate would-be passenger. A newsboy in front of the Independent
Subway entrance. 'Trouble in the Middle East! Evening papers! Get
your trouble in the Middle East!'*

INT. LOBBY OF OFFICE BUILDING — MADISON AVENUE

*Four elevators in action. A starter keeping things humming. Doors close
on an elevator. It starts up. Another elevator arrives at street level. The
last credit fades. The elevator doors open. Crowds pour out, and we hear
a voice at the rear of the car even before the man is revealed to us by the
off-going passengers. He is Roger Thornhill, tall, lean, faultlessly dressed
(and far too original to be wearing the gray-flannel uniform of his
kind). He has been dictating to his secretary, Maggie, an ageing,
unbeautiful woman who has accompanied him down in the elevator
with pad and pencil in hand. She will have to scurry to keep up with his
impatient stride when they leave the elevator and cross the lobby to the
entrance.*

THORNHILL
(*dictating*)

. . . Even if you accept the belief that a high Trendex
automatically means a rising sales curve, which incidentally I
do *not* accept . . .
(*to elevator starter*)
'Night, Eddie.

STARTER

Mr Thornhill.

3

THORNHILL

Say hello to the missus.

STARTER
(*sourly*)

We're not talking.

THORNHILL
(*to Maggie, continuing dictation as they cross lobby*)
My recommendation is still the same. Dash. Spread the good
word in as many small-time segments as we can grab . . .
(*as he pauses at the news-stand, buys a paper*)
. . . And let the opposition have their high ratings, while we
cry about it all the way to the bank.
(*moving on*)
Why don't we colonize at the Colony one day next week for
lunch? Let me hear from you, Sam. Happy thoughts.
Etcetera . . .
(*they are at the entrance now*)
Better walk me to the Plaza.

MAGGIE
(*a weary moan*)

Walk?

THORNHILL

Use your blood sugar. Come on.

He eases her through the door, follows her to the sidewalk.

EXT. STREET – TRACKING SHOT

They start to walk west, Thornhill glancing at the newspaper as he goes.

THORNHILL

Next?

MAGGIE
(*consulting her pad*)

Gretchen Sabinson.

THORNHILL
(*grimaces*)
Send her a box of candy from Blum's. Ten dollars. The kind

4

. . . you know . . . each piece wrapped in gold paper? She'll
like that. She'll think she's eating money. Say: 'Darling, I
count the days, the hours, the minutes –'

> MAGGIE
> (*interrupting*)

You sent that one last time.

> THORNHILL

Did I? Then just say: 'Something for your sweet tooth, honey
. . . and all your other sweet parts.'
> (*Maggie gives him a look and he winces*)

I know, I know.

> MAGGIE

Could we take a cab, Mr Thornhill?

> THORNHILL

A couple of blocks?

> MAGGIE

You're late and I'm tired.

> THORNHILL

I keep telling you, Maggie, you don't eat properly.
> (*steps off the curb, tries to flag a cab*)

Taxi! . . . Taxi!

*He is getting nowhere. Just then, a taxi pulls up before a man who has
also been seeking one. Quickly Thornhill darts over and opens the door.*

> (*to the man*)

I have a sick woman here. Would you mind terribly?

> MAN
> (*a little bewildered*)

Why no . . . I mean –

> THORNHILL
> (*quickly*)

Thank you very much.

*He quickly bundles Maggie into the cab, follows her in and slams the
door shut.*

MAN
(still befuddled)
Perfectly all right . . .

The cab pulls away.

INT. CAB

THORNHILL
(to driver)
First stop, the Plaza. Don't throw the flag.

MAGGIE
(looking back)
Poor man.

THORNHILL
Poor man nothing. I made him a Good Samaritan.

MAGGIE
He knew you were lying.

THORNHILL
(opening up the newspaper again)
In the world of advertising there is no such thing as a lie, Maggie. There is only The Expedient Exaggeration. Do I look a little heavyish to you?

MAGGIE
What?

THORNHILL
I *feel* heavyish. Put a note on my desk in the morning. 'Think thin.'

MAGGIE
(writing)
Think thin.

THORNHILL
(to the driver)
Make it the Fifty-ninth Street entrance, driver.

6

                              DRIVER
Okay.

                            THORNHILL
        (*to Maggie, as he continues to peruse the newspaper*)
Soon as you get back to the office, call my mother, tell her
about the theatre tickets for tonight. Dinner at Twenty-One,
seven o'clock. I'll have had two Martinis at the Oak Bar, so
she needn't bother to sniff me.

                             MAGGIE
She doesn't do *that*.

                            THORNHILL
Like a bloodhound.

As the cab pulls up before the Fifty-ninth Street entrance to the Plaza:

                             MAGGIE
                       (*reading from notes*)
Bigelow at ten-thirty is your first for tomorrow. You're due at
the Skin Glow rehearsal at noon. Then lunch with Falcon and
his wife –

                            THORNHILL
                    (*handing her some money*)
Oh, yes. Where was that?

                             MAGGIE
Larry and Arnold's. One o'clock.

*Thornhill has dropped his newspaper on the seat and is on his way out
of the cab.*

Will you check in later?

EXT. PLAZA HOTEL

                            THORNHILL
                      (*now out of the cab*)
Absolutely not.
                          (*to driver*)
Take this lady back where she belongs.

                               7

DRIVER

Right.

THORNHILL
(*to Maggie*)
Don't forget to call my mother right away.

MAGGIE
I won't. Goodnight, Mr Thornhill.

Thornhill slams the door and the cab starts away. Suddenly he remembers something, snaps his fingers, points after the cab.

THORNHILL
Wait a minute! You *can't* call her! She's at Mrs –

He stops. The cab is already on its way. He stands there for a moment looking after it. Then he goes up the steps into the hotel.

INT. LOBBY PLAZA HOTEL

Thornhill glances at his wrist-watch as he crosses the lobby to the Oak Bar.

INT. OAK BAR

Thornhill pauses in the entrance, looking about impatiently. The Captain comes up to him.

CAPTAIN
Evening, Mr Thornhill.

THORNHILL
Hello, Victor. I'm looking for Herman Weltner and two gentlemen –

CAPTAIN
(*pointing*)
Yes. Right over there.

THORNHILL
Oh yes.

Thornhill walks to a far corner of the room to the table where Weltner, an Ivy-League costumed executive, is seated with a Mr Nelson and a

Mr Wade, both of whom look like out-of-town sponsors, which they are.

> WELTNER
> (*rising to his feet*)

Roger.

> THORNHILL
> (*shaking his hand*)

Herman. Sorry I'm so late.

> WELTNER
> (*making introductions*)

This is Roger Thornhill. Fanning Nelson –

Nelson cups a hand to his ear.

> THORNHILL
> (*shaking his other hand*)

Delighted.

> WELTNER

And Larry Wade.

> THORNHILL
> (*shaking hands*)

How do you do, Mr Wade?

> WADE
> (*indicating his drink*)

We've gotten a little head start here, Mr Thornhill.

> THORNHILL

Won't last for long.

He sits down, looking about nervously.

> WELTNER

I was just telling Larry and Fanning here that you may be slow in starting but there's nobody faster down the homestretch.
> (*noting Thornhill's nervousness*)
What's the matter, Roger? You've got the fidgets.

During the following, a Bellboy will enter the room and move among the tables calling out: 'Paging Mr George Kaplan!' *Standing in the entrance watching the Bellboy's progress (and observed by us if we happen to be looking off into background) are two rather unobtrusive-looking Men:*

THORNHILL

Something very silly. I told my secretary to call my mother, and I just remembered, she's not going to be able to reach her in time.

WELTNER

Why not?

THORNHILL

Because she's playing bridge at the apartment of one of her cronies . . .

WELTNER

Your secretary?

THORNHILL

No. My mother. And it's one of those brand-new apartments – all wet paint and no telephone yet.

NELSON
(*cupping his ear*)

What was that?

Thornhill looks at him with astonishment.

BELLBOY
(*approaching*)

Paging Mr George Kaplan!

THORNHILL
(*musing*)

I think maybe if I send her a telegram . . .

BELLBOY
(*closer*)

Mr George Kaplan!

> THORNHILL
> (*signaling the boy*)
> Boy – would you come here please?

CUT TO:

CLOSE ANGLE: THE TWO MEN STANDING IN ENTRANCE TO ROOM
They react with sudden interest, glance at each other, then look off again and see:

POINT OF VIEW: FROM ENTRANCE
The Bellboy moving up to Thornhill, whose table is well out of earshot of the entrance.

CLOSE ANGLE: THE TABLE
Thornhill takes a pen and a long envelope from his inside pocket as he addresses the Bellboy:

> THORNHILL
> Look, I've got to get a wire off immediately. Can you send it for me if I write it out for you?

> BELLBOY
> I'm not permitted to do that, sir, but if you'll follow me –

> THORNHILL
> (*to the others at the table*)
> Will you excuse me for a moment?

> WADE
> Go right ahead.

> NELSON
> (*cupping his ear*)
> What was that?

Thornhill gives him a quick look.

> THORNHILL
> (*to Weltner, as he gets up*)
> Herman, if you can scare up a double Martini . . .

WELTNER

Sure thing.

Thornhill walks off with the Bellboy.

NELSON
(*turning to Wade*)

Where's he going?

WADE

There's no telephone where his mother is playing bridge.

NELSON
(*stares at him a moment*)

Why not?

Now Wade *gives him a look.*

OUTSIDE THE OAK BAR

Thornhill and the Bellboy emerge from the room.

BELLBOY
(*pointing*)

Right there, sir.

THORNHILL
(*giving him a tip*)

Thanks.

BELLBOY

Thank *you*, sir.

Thornhill starts towards the Western Union office, as the Bellboy goes off in another direction. Suddenly the two 'unobtrusive' Men walk swiftly into the shot directly behind Thornhill. One of them, who we now see has a scar on the corner of his right eye, *taps him on the shoulder. He pauses and turns.*

THORNHILL

Yes?

FIRST MAN
(*with a faint foreign accent*)
The car is waiting outside. You will walk between us saying
nothing.

THORNHILL
What are you talking about?

SECOND MAN
(*taking Thornhill's arm*)
Let's go.

THORNHILL
Go where? Who *are* you?

FIRST MAN
Mere errand boys, carrying concealed weapons. His is pointed
at your heart, so, please, no errors of judgement, I beg of you.

THORNHILL
(*pulling free*)
What is this – a joke or something?

SECOND MAN
Yes. A joke.
(*he removes his hand from his pocket, shoves a gun into
Thornhill's ribs*)
We will laugh in the car.

Thornhill stares at the man for a moment.

THORNHILL
This is ridiculous.

*The Man nods towards the side entrance and Thornhill starts away,
flanked on either side.*

EXT. STREET

*Thornhill emerges from the hotel to the sidewalk. The Men take his
arms and ease him inconspicuously past unnoticing passersby to a
limousine parked at the curb. They open the rear door, push Thornhill
into the back seat and follow him in. A third Man sitting behind the
wheel immediately starts the car and pulls away.*

13

INT. CAR

As the car moves east, Thornhill glances at the stony-faced men on either side of him. He is anxious, but does not want to show it.

> **THORNHILL**
> Don't tell me where we're going. Surprise me.

The Men stare straight ahead, saying nothing.

> Y'know, I left some people waiting for me back there in the Oak Bar, and they're going to think I'm awfully rude, going off like this.
> *(he waits – no response)*
> I mean, if you could let me off at a drugstore for a moment, I could call and explain that I'm . . .
> *(he glances at the men inquiringly)*
> . . . being . . . kidnapped?
> *(no response)*
> That *is* what's happening, isn't it?

No answer. His glance goes to the door handle. The car has stopped for a red light. Suddenly he lunges for the door and struggles to open it, as the two Men watch him calmly. Apparently the door has special locks. It will not budge. Thornhill takes his seat again and points sheepishly to the door.

> Locked.

DISSOLVE TO:

EXT. GLEN COVE ESTATE – DUSK

The car approaches the entrance to a magnificent estate. On the open gate, a nameplate: TOWNSEND. *The car turns into the driveway.*

INT. CAR

Thornhill, flanked by the two Men, is looking over his shoulder at the receding gates. He turns forward, looks at one of the Men.

> **THORNHILL**
> Who's Townsend?

*No answer. He glances at the other man questioningly. More stony
silence.*

Oh, really? Interesting.

Then he looks out ahead.

MOVING POINT OF VIEW

A curving, tree-lined driveway. Through the trees, a red-brick mansion.

INT. CAR

Thornhill is still looking out.

EXT. MAIN HOUSE

*An impressive though considerably faded mansion of the early twenties.
The car swings around the circular driveway, pulls up before the
entrance. Thornhill and the two Men get out. One of the Men (he of the
scarred eye – his name is Valerian) accompanies Thornhill up the steps
to the front door. The other man (Licht) follows them and waits until
the door opens before he moves away and follows a path to the rear of
the house. After a moment, a stocky, gray-haired woman wearing the
uniform of a Housekeeper opens the front door. Valerian walks
Thornhill right in past her.*

INT. HOUSE

*Beyond the oval foyer, a curving marble staircase leads to a balcony, off
which are many rooms. Above the balcony, a stained-glass window.
Everywhere, a kind of seedy grandeur.*

> VALERIAN
> (*to housekeeper*)

Where is he?

> HOUSEKEEPER

Upstairs, dressing.

> VALERIAN

Tell him I'm here.

HOUSEKEEPER

The dinner guests are expected.

VALERIAN
(*impatiently*)

Never mind. Say to him 'Kaplan'.

At this, the woman glances at Thornhill.

THORNHILL

By the way – what are we having for dessert?

VALERIAN
(*to Housekeeper*)

Is anyone in the library?

HOUSEKEEPER

No.

VALERIAN
(*to Thornhill, brusquely*)

This way.

He walks Thornhill to the library door, as the Housekeeper goes upstairs.

INT. LIBRARY

Books, from floor to ceiling. And windows overlooking the rear lawn. In the distance, Long Island Sound. Valerian opens the door, gestures to Thornhill, who enters.

VALERIAN
(*his hand on the key*)

You will wait here.

THORNHILL
(*indicating the shelves of books*)

Don't hurry. I'll catch up on my reading.

Valerian closes the door behind him. Immediately, Thornhill goes to the door to open it. Just as his hand reaches the knob, he hears the door being locked from the outside. He tries it anyway, then turns, glances around, walks to the desk, sees several magazines there: Field and Stream . . . Newsweek . . . Fortune . . . *etc.* In an INSERT, *he and* we see that the addressee on all of them is: 'Mr Lester Townsend, Baywood, Glen Cove, NY'. *Thornhill steps to a window, peers out.*

EXT. BACK LAWN

THORNHILL'S POINT OF VIEW: *a man is playing croquet all by himself in the fading light. His name is Leonard. Later, we will see him at closer range. He is about thirty, but looks much younger, for he has a soft baby-face, large eyes and hair that falls down over his forehead. His attitudes are unmistakably effeminate. Hurrying towards him is Licht, the other abductor. In a brief pantomime, Licht apparently gives Leonard tidings, and they quickly go off together towards the house.*

INT. LIBRARY

Seeing the back lawn now deserted, Thornhill tries to open the window to escape. It is locked. He unfastens the catch, raises the window, is about to climb out when he draws back and turns at the sound of the door opening behind him. In walks a distinguished looking Man of about forty, professorial in manner but definitely sexually attractive (to women), and only slightly sinister.

> MAN
> *(affably)*
> Good evening . . .

He holds out his hand. Thornhill takes it uncertainly.

> THORNHILL
> Not a moment too soon.

> MAN
> *(scrutinizing him)*
> Well – so . . .

> THORNHILL
> Thank you. That explains everything.

> MAN
> *(still peering at him)*
> . . . Not what I expected – a little taller, a little more polished than the others . . .

THORNHILL
(*with bite*)
I'm so glad you're pleased, Mr Townsend.

MAN
(*reacts, then smiles*)
. . . But I'm afraid just as obvious.

THORNHILL
Forgive me for being obvious, but what the devil is this all
about? Why was I brought here?

MAN
(*wearily*)
Games? . . . Must we?

THORNHILL
Not that I mind a slight case of abduction now and then, but
I do have tickets to the theatre tonight and it was a show I was
looking forward to and I get, well, kind of *unreasonable* about
things like that.

MAN
With such expert play-acting, you make this very room a theatre.
(*the man of the croquet wickets enters*)
Ah – Leonard. Have you met our distinguished guest?

LEONARD
(*staring at Thornhill*)
He's a well-tailored one, isn't he?

Thornhill gives him a look of distaste.

MAN
My secretary is a great admirer of your methods, Mr Kaplan.
Elusiveness, however misguided –

THORNHILL
(*interrupting*)
Wait a minute. Did you call me Kaplan?

MAN
Oh, I know you're a man of many names, but I'm perfectly
willing to accept your current choice.

THORNHILL

Current choice? My name is Thornhill – Roger Thornhill –
and it's never been anything else.

MAN

Of course . . .

Leonard starts to chuckle.

THORNHILL
(*smiling*)

Obviously your friends picked up the wrong package when
they bundled me out here in the car.

MAN
(*tired of all this*)

Sit down, Mr Kaplan, won't you?

THORNHILL
(*the smile fades*)

I told you: I'm not Kaplan, whoever *he* is. I'm Roger
Thornhill of the Wadley and Rapp Agency, and unless you
gentlemen happen to be interested in *advertising* something,
this meeting is going to turn out to be an enormous bust for
all concerned.

*There is a knock on the door. It opens and a handsome Woman in her
forties peers in.*

WOMAN

Excuse me –

MAN
(*politely*)

Yes?

WOMAN

The guests are here.

MAN

Look after them. I'll be with you in a few minutes.

THORNHILL
(*turning on her with sarcasm*)
Don't bother to set a place for me, Mrs Townsend. I won't be staying for dinner.

She gives a flustered glance in the direction of the men, then hurriedly withdraws, and closes the door.

MAN
(*to Thornhill*)
Now – shall we get down to business?

THORNHILL
I'm all for that.

MAN
Quite simply, I'd like you to tell me how much you know of our arrangements and – of course – how you've *come* by this information. Naturally, I don't expect to get this for nothing.

THORNHILL
(*with a sarcastic bow of the head*)
Of course not.

MAN
Don't misunderstand me. I don't really expect you to fall in with my suggestion, but the least I can do is afford you the opportunity of surviving the evening –

THORNHILL
(*frowns*)
Surviving the evening . . .?

MAN
Now why don't you surprise me, Mr Kaplan, and say 'yes'?

THORNHILL
I already told you –

LEONARD
(*interrupting*)
We know where you're headed for . . .

THORNHILL
(*turning on him*)
I'm headed for the Winter Garden Theatre in New York, and
I think I better get going.

*He goes to the door, flings it open, sees Valerian standing there blocking
the entrance. He turns.*

Townsend – you're making a serious mistake . . .

*Leonard eases over and closes the door again as the Man, walking to
the desk, says:*

MAN
This is not going to lead to a very happy conclusion, Mr
Kaplan –

THORNHILL
I'm not Kaplan!

MAN
I do wish you would reconsider.

LEONARD
We also know your contact in Pittsburgh since Jason
committed suicide.

THORNHILL
(*angrily*)
What contact? I've never even *been* in Pittsburgh.

*The other Man is at the desk, looking down at a piece of paper as he
speaks quickly:*

MAN
On June sixteenth, you checked into the Sherwyn Hotel in
Pittsburgh as Mr George Kaplan of Berkeley, California. A
week later you registered at the Benjamin Franklin Hotel in
Philadelphia as Mr George Kaplan of Pittsburgh. On August
eleventh you stayed at the Statler in Boston. On August
twenty-ninth George Kaplan of Boston registered at the
Whittier in Detroit. At present, you are registered in room
seven ninety-six at the Plaza Hotel in New York as Mr
George Kaplan of Detroit –

                    THORNHILL
                     (*tersely*)
What else?

                      MAN
– In two days, you are due at the Ambassador East in
Chicago –

                    THORNHILL
Oh?

                      MAN
– And then at the Sheraton-Johnson Hotel in Rapid City,
South Dakota.

                    THORNHILL
                  (*shaking his head*)
Not me.

                      MAN
– So you see, there is little sense in maintaining this fiction
that you are deceiving us, any more than *we* are deceiving *you*,
Mr Kaplan.

Thornhill stares at him for a long moment, helplessly frustrated.

                    THORNHILL
I don't suppose it would do any good to show you a wallet
full of identification cards, a driver's license, things like that?

                     LEONARD
                  (*shakes his head*)
They provide you with such *good* ones.

                      MAN
                     (*quietly*)
It's getting late. Do you intend to cooperate with us? I'd like a
simple yes or no.

                    THORNHILL
                (*completely exasperated*)
All right. A simple no. For the simple reason that I simply
don't know what you're talking about.

MAN
(*turns to his secretary*)
Give Mr Kaplan a drink, Leonard.
(*he turns to Thornhill*)
A pleasant journey, sir.

The Man goes to the door, opens it, holds it open for a fraction.
Valerian and Licht enter. The Man leaves, closing the door behind him.
Leonard opens a cabinet. Liquor bottles are seen. He turns to Thornhill.

LEONARD
Scotch? Rye? Bourbon? Vodka?

THORNHILL
Nothing. I'll just take a quick ride back to town.

LEONARD
That has been arranged . . .

Thornhill glances at the deadpan faces of Valerian and Licht with
growing apprehension.

But first, a libation.

Leonard reaches into the cabinet, takes out a large bottle of whiskey. He
holds it up.

Bourbon.

He moves towards Thornhill with the bottle.

THORNHILL
You have some. I've had enough stimulation for one day.

LEONARD
(*gently*)
It will be easier if you take this yourself. Otherwise, it will be
necessary for us to insist.

Thornhill's eyes widen. He points at the bottle.

THORNHILL
The whole quart?

LEONARD
Not a quart, Mr Kaplan. It's only a fifth.

23

Thornhill makes a sudden move, tries to go past him to the door, but Valerian and Licht grab him, pin his arms behind him. As they do so, camera dollies in to a full head and shoulders shot of Thornhill, who stares off screen. We hear the pop of the cork being drawn from the bottle. Then Leonard's hand comes up into the shot holding an empty tumbler.

LEONARD'S VOICE
(*off-screen*)

Cheers.

Now the bottle comes into shot and begins to fill the tumbler with bourbon before Thornhill's staring face.

DISSOLVE TO:

EXT. HILL ROAD – NIGHT

Two cars are making their way along a winding, precipitous road. The leading car is a light-colored open Mercedes Benz. Behind it is the limousine which brought Thornhill from the Plaza Hotel to Glen Cove. We hear Thornhill's voice coming from the leading car in drunken song:

'*Somewhere I'll find you . . . Sneak up behind you . . .*' *The two cars come to a stop at the top of the hill. The driver of the limousine gets out quickly and we see that it is Licht. He crosses over swiftly to the Mercedes Benz.*

CLOSE ANGLE: THE MERCEDES BENZ
The driver of the Mercedes Benz – Valerian – is just getting out as Licht arrives. Sitting in the Mercedes Benz, mumbling and singing drunkenly, is Thornhill.

> THORNHILL
> (*with gestures*)
> G'night Mr Townsend . . . Mizz Townsend . . . 'night . . .
> Parting such sweet sorrow . . .
> (*sings*)
> 'I've grown accustomed to your . . . bourbon . . .'

During this, the two Men have held a brief, sharp exchange in a foreign tongue. Valerian takes a quick step towards the edge and sees:

POINT OF VIEW
The winding, descending, precipitous road ahead.

CLOSE ANGLE: THE MERCEDES BENZ
Valerian turns back and with the help of Licht hurriedly pulls Thornhill into the driver's seat. Then, as Licht runs to the limousine, Valerian gets into the Mercedes Benz beside Thornhill, reaches across and starts the motor.

> THORNHILL
> (*mumbles*)
> Don't worry about me, fellahs. I'll take the bus from here.

INT. MERCEDES BENZ

Valerian releases the handbrake, pushes Thornhill back, takes the wheel and applies his left foot to the accelerator. As the car starts to move, Valerian glances ahead tensely.

POINT OF VIEW
The car is approaching a precipice.

INT. MERCEDES BENZ

Valerian opens the door at his side and gets ready to jump. Just then, Thornhill, opening a bleary eye, begins to sense what is happening. He turns, puts both hands on Valerian and gives him a violent shove, saying thickly:

THORNHILL
You take the bus too.

Valerian falls out of the car. Thornhill grabs the wheel and turns it sharply.

EXT. MERCEDES BENZ

The outside wheels travel along the edge of the precipice.

THORNHILL AT THE WHEEL
Looks ahead, only slightly aware of his danger. He gives the wheel another wrench.

CLOSE-UP: MERCEDES BENZ
The rear outside wheel is over the edge, spins in mid-air for a moment. Then the inner wheel gets a grip on the crumbling edge, and the car shoots forward.

CLOSE-UP: THORNHILL AT THE WHEEL
He turns, glances back, sees:

POINT OF VIEW:
Valerian in the act of getting into the already moving limousine.

EXT. MERCEDES BENZ

It picks up speed and goes careening down the winding, precipitous road.

EXT. LIMOUSINE

Valerian and Licht are in hot and angry pursuit.

THE CHASE SEQUENCE

The Mercedes Benz can take the sharp curves with more ease than the limousine. Also, Thornhill is too far gone to know that he shouldn't drive that fast. Consequently, he gets to the foot of the hill and down to a main thoroughfare still in the lead. Naturally, we film this ride, and that which follows, from many different angles, including Thornhill's delirious double-vision point of view. He will be killed if he is caught, and he will be killed if he keeps driving this way. There is very little choice really. On the highway now, he is doing eighty, weaving wildly through traffic, swerving suicidally over double lanes and giving heart failure to oncoming truck drivers. But he is leaving the limousine behind.

A POLICE CAR

Two Officers in the front seat. The car is travelling along at a normal speed. Suddenly Thornhill's car comes dashing by. The officers react immediately, start in pursuit.

INT. LIMOUSINE

Valerian and Licht see the police car, which is almost directly in front of them, take off after Thornhill. Valerian signals to Licht to slow down. Licht does so, and starts to make a U-turn.

INT. THE MERCEDES BENZ

Thornhill tries desperately to keep his eyes in focus, his foot on the floorboard and his hands on the wheel. Horns blare warningly as he comes perilously close to several head-on crashes. In his rear-view mirror, he sees the headlights of the police car following and does not realize that it is no longer the limousine. The headlights are coming closer. Suddenly, almost too late, he sees ahead of him an elderly gentleman on a bicycle emerge from a side road. He slams on the brakes and the car comes to a screaming, wobbling stop. The bicyclist, oblivious, continues across.

SIDE ANGLE

As Thornhill's car comes to a final, jerking halt, the police car, with screaming brakes, hits Thornhill's rear. There is a crunching sound as the bonnet of the police car crumples like tin. There is a momentary silence and then the sudden scream of more brakes, and a third car smashes into the back of the police car, giving it a crumpled rear *as well. Thornhill drunkenly leans out and looks behind to see what all the fuss is about. The two Police Officers, after forcing a door open, emerge, glowering. At the same time, the third driver is seen getting out of his car, somewhat bewildered, and starting forward.*

DISSOLVE TO:

INT. GLEN COVE POLICE STATION – NIGHT

A Lieutenant Hagerman is behind the desk. To his right is a radiophone transmitter-receiver, over which we hear the faint communications of cruising police cars and their patrol stations. A commotion is heard outside, and then one of the police-car Officers, a gentleman known as Sergeant Klinger, escorts a wobbly Thornhill into the building.

> THORNHILL
> (*thickly*)
> Thanks for the lift, fellahs.

> KLINGER
> Lieutenant – I want this man examined for driving while intoxicated.

> LIEUTENANT
> (*looking at the swaying Thornhill*)
> Really?

> THORNHILL
> (*to the lieutenant*)
> They tried to kill me . . . He won't listen . . . Big house . . . They tried to kill me.

> KLINGER
> (*during above*)
> All right. Let's just go inside . . .

> THORNHILL
> (*moving with him*)
> Don't wanna go inside. Somebody call the police.

28

The Sergeant leads Thornhill by the arm into the courtroom.

INT. COURTROOM

A bleak room at this late hour of night.

> KLINGER
> *(indicating a chair)*
>
> Sit down.

> THORNHILL
>
> Don't wanna sit. Perfectly all right.
> *(he falls into the seat)*
> We'll throw the book at 'em. Kidnapping. Assault with gun
> . . . and bourbon . . . and sports car. *We'll* get 'em.

> KLINGER
>
> You'll be all right after a good night's sleep. We got a nice cell
> all made up and waiting.

> THORNHILL
>
> Don't wanna cell. I want a policeman.

The other arresting officer, Patrolman Waggoner, enters.

> WAGGONER
>
> The car was just reported stolen.

> KLINGER
>
> Uh huh.

> WAGGONER
>
> A Mrs Babson up on Twining Road.

> THORNHILL
> *(getting unsteadily to his feet)*
> Gotta call someone. Where's the phone?

> KLINGER
>
> You're allowed one call. Right over here.
> *(leads Thornhill to a nearby phone)*
> Better make it your lawyer.

THORNHILL
(*to Klinger*)
Butterfield eight-one-oh-nine-eight.

KLINGER
What am I – a telephone operator?

THORNHILL
(*nodding*)
Yeah. Butterfield eight-one-oh-nine-eight.

Reluctantly, Klinger puts the call through. After a few moments:

KLINGER
(*to phone*)
Just a minute please . . . Here.

He hands the phone to Thornhill.

THORNHILL
(*to phone*)
Hello, Mother? This is your son, Roger Thornhill.
(*listens*)
Wait a minute.
(*to Klinger*)
Where am I?

KLINGER
Glen Cove Police Station.

THORNHILL
(*to phone*)
Glen Cove Police Station . . .
(*listens*)
Now is that a nice thing to say, Mother? I have *not* been
drinking again. But these two fellows poured a bottle of
bourbon down my throat –
(*listens, shakes his head*)
No. They didn't give me a chaser . . .

*During above, Dr Cross, a pleasant young physician, has entered.
Klinger comes over, interrupts Thornhill.*

Wait a minute, Mother.

                         (*to Klinger*)
Not finished yet.

                         KLINGER
Yes you are. C'mon.

                         THORNHILL
                         (*to phone*)
Gotta hang up now, Mother. You better get my lawyer right
away and bail me out.

                         KLINGER
Tomorrow morning, tell her.

                         THORNHILL
                         (*to phone*)
He says 'tomorrow morning'.
                         (*listens*)
I don't know. I'll ask him.
                         (*to Klinger*)
She wants to know *who* says.

                         KLINGER
Sergeant Emil Klinger

                         THORNHILL
                         (*to phone*)
Sergeant Emil –
                         (*a double take at the Sergeant*)
Emil?
                         (*to phone*)
Sergeant Emil Klinger.
                         (*listens*)
No. I didn't believe it either.
                         (*listens*)
Don't worry. I'm all right, Mother. 'Nightie night.
                         (*he hangs up*)
That was Mother.

*Klinger leads him over to a table where Dr Cross is waiting with
medical kit.*

> KLINGER
> *(to Dr Cross)*
Here's your man, Doctor.

Cross glances at Thornhill, indicates a chair. Thornhill collapses into it. Klinger and Patrolman Waggoner move into background as silent observers. Cross takes out a questionnaire and a fountain pen, begins to fill out the form, quickly and perfunctorily.

> DR CROSS
What's your name?

> THORNHILL
Roger Thornhill. Don't believe we've met.

> DR CROSS
Address?

> THORNHILL
Eighty-four Sutton Place. Doctor, you listen to me –

> DR CROSS
Were you operating the motor vehicle in question?

> THORNHILL
Admirably.

> DR CROSS
Where were you going?

> THORNHILL
No place. Just trying to get away from some fellahs who were trying to kill me. I've been trying to tell these –

> DR CROSS
Where did you start from?

> THORNHILL
Big house. I don't know where. Big house. And these fellahs –

> DR CROSS
> *(interrupting)*
Stand up please, Mr Thornhill . . .

THORNHILL
(*struggling to his feet*)
Sure.

DR CROSS
(*throwing some coins on the floor*)
. . . And pick up those coins.

THORNHILL
(*looking right at the money*)
What coins?

DR CROSS
(*pointing to a white line on the floor*)
Never mind. Now I want you to walk that line.

THORNHILL
(*as he tries unsuccessfully to negotiate the line*)
At first I thought they were gonna hold me for ransom. They brought me to this house. Can't remember the guy's name right now. Think it was Kaplan. Yeah, George Kaplan –

He stops abruptly as he falls to the floor. Then, as he starts to get to his feet again:

DR CROSS
Ever have diabetes?

THORNHILL
Never touch the stuff.

DR CROSS
'Then you're not taking insulin.

THORNHILL
Never touch the stuff.

DR CROSS
Have you used a mouthwash recently?

THORNHILL
Never stuch the tuff.

DR CROSS
Stick out your tongue and say 'ah'.

THORNHILL
Better move back . . . Ah-h-h!

DR CROSS
Have you been drinking?

THORNHILL
Doctor – I am gassed.

DR CROSS
What were you drinking?

THORNHILL
Bourbon. They held me down and another guy –

DR CROSS
How much would you say you drank?

THORNHILL
(*holding his palms about a foot apart*)
About this much.

He starts towards a long table as:

DR CROSS
Mr Thornhill – it is my opinion that you are definitely
intoxicated . . .
(*as Thornhill lies down on the table*)
. . . And I am now going to have to ask your permission to
draw blood.

THORNHILL
(*a sleepy murmur*)
How disgusting.

DR CROSS
(*reading very quickly from his questionnaire*)
'You may refuse to permit a blood test to be made, but if you
do refuse, your license will be revoked. You have the right to
notify a physician of your own choosing to administer this
chemical test if you so prefer.'
(*looking up*)
Is that understood, Mr Thornhill?
(*no response*)

Mr Thornhill?

Sergeant Klinger steps forward, puts a finger to his lips.

KLINGER
Shhh . . .

He looks down at Thornhill with mock tenderness. Now we see Thornhill. He is sleeping like a baby, with a little smile on his face.

DISSOLVE TO:

INT. COURTROOM – NEXT MORNING

The judge, Anson B. Flynn, is staring coldly down at Thornhill, who, looking plenty the worse for a night in jail, stands between his attorney, Victor Larrabee, and Sergeant Klinger. Seated behind them is Thornhill's mother, Clara Thornhill, a woman who has played so much bridge she is getting to look like the Queen of Hearts. During the following, Thornhill turns, smiles at her feebly. She does not smile back:

LARRABEE
(*speaking with ill-concealed distaste*)
– It was at this point that Mr Thornhill succeeded in *escaping* from his would-be assassins, and when they gave chase, he, naturally, had to drive as best he could under the, uh, circumstances. But unfortunately the, uh, circumstances were a little more than he could handle, and so, well, here we are.

THORNHILL
(*half aloud*)
But where are *they*?

The judge gives Thornhill a hard-eyed look, then turns to Larrabee.

JUDGE
Counsellor, how long have you known your client?

LARRABEE
Seven years, Your Honor.

JUDGE
Do you know him to be a reasonable man?

35

LARRABEE

Absolutely.

In background, Mrs Thornhill gives an audible sniff of scorn. Thornhill quickly turns and gives her an angry whisper.

THORNHILL

Mother!

JUDGE

And do you believe there is some credence to this . . . story?

THORNHILL
(bridling)

Credence!

LARRABEE

Well . . . yes, Your Honor. I mean if my client says that this is what happened, I am certain it must have . . .
(he shrugs)
. . . happened.

JUDGE

Mm hmm.
(he turns to Klinger)
Sergeant – I want this turned over to the County Detectives for investigation. I suggest you call them up and have them come over here immediately.

KLINGER
(starting away)

Right, Your Honor.

JUDGE

Counsellor, I'm going to set this over for final disposition tomorrow night at seven-thirty, at which time I expect you and the defendant to be here and ready to go to trial. In the meantime, the County Detectives will determine whether his story has any basis in fact –

THORNHILL
(indignantly)

Basis in fact? I suppose if I were brought in here *dead*, you *still* wouldn't believe – !

LARRABEE
(*interrupting*)
Now, Roger, wait a minute!

THORNHILL
I mean, after all, Your Honor, would I make *up* such a story?

JUDGE
That is precisely what we intend to find out, Mr Thornhill.

DISSOLVE TO:

EXT. GLEN COVE ROAD – DAY

The County Detectives' Car, a plain black sedan, is cruising in the tree-lined 'estate' area of Glen Cove.

INT. CAR

Two detectives are up front – Lieutenant Harding and Captain Junket. In the back seat, Thornhill is quietly arguing with his mother while Victor Larrabee listens in strained silence.

THORNHILL
. . . Because any drinking I do to excess, Mother dear, can be attributed only to the bad example set by my immediate ancestors. You are not exactly, may I remind you, addicted to *homogenized milk.*

MRS THORNHILL
Sometimes I wonder why I stand for your impertinences.

THORNHILL
You wouldn't have to if you could learn to cheat at bridge.
(*an aside to Larrabee*)
I support *all* her girl friends.

LARRABEE
Now, now, Roger . . .

MRS THORNHILL
(*scoffing*)
Not *Roger*. You forget. It's *George*.

37

> (*she chuckles*)
George Kaplan.

                    CAPTAIN JUNKET
                      (*turning*)
Here's the Townsend estate. Look familiar?

                      THORNHILL
                    (*looking out*)
Yeah. That's it.

EXT. THE CAR — TRAVELLING SHOT

The car enters the estate through the open gates, proceeds along the curving driveway and finally comes to a stop before the entrance to the main house.

EXT. MAIN HOUSE

Everyone in the car gets out. The detectives lead the way to the front door and ring the bell. Presently the door is opened by the Housekeeper, who seems not at all perturbed to see the group standing before her.

                     HOUSEKEEPER
                    (*pleasantly*)
Yes?

                      THORNHILL
Remember me?

                     HOUSEKEEPER
Yes, sir.

                      THORNHILL
                 (*satisfied, but grim*)
Good.

                    CAPTAIN JUNKET
Is Mr Townsend at home?

                     HOUSEKEEPER
No, I'm sorry, sir. He's left for the day.

                    CAPTAIN JUNKET
Mrs Townsend?

                    HOUSEKEEPER
                    (*after a pause*)
Who shall I tell her is calling?

                    CAPTAIN JUNKET
County detectives.

                    HOUSEKEEPER
                    (*unperturbed*)
Come in, please.

She opens the door wider.

INT. HOUSE

They all enter.

                    HOUSEKEEPER
This way, please.

She leads them to the library, opens the door for them and they enter.

INT. LIBRARY

                    THORNHILL
This is the room.

                    HOUSEKEEPER
I'll call madam.

                    CAPTAIN JUNKET
You do that.

The Housekeeper withdraws. Thornhill points to the settee.

                    THORNHILL
There's the sofa.
                    (*going to the sofa*)
They spilled bourbon all over it. I'll show you the stains.

He examines the seat cushion, frowns, turns the cushion over, frowns even more deeply. He looks up. Everyone is staring at him. He turns, looks about, spies the liquor cabinet.

There's where they kept the liquor! Scotch and gin and vodka – !

MRS THORNHILL
And bourbon.

Thornhill goes over, whips open the cabinet. It is filled with books. No liquor. Just books.

I remember when it used to come in bottles.

Just then the handsome Woman of the night before enters, beaming graciously and talking very fast as she goes to Thornhill.

WOMAN
Roger! Dear!
> (*he straightens up, astounded*)

We were so worried about you! Did you get home all right?
> (*she embraces him*)

Of course you did. Let me look at you. A little pink-eyed and fuzzy around the cheeks. But then, aren't we all? It was a dull party really, and you didn't miss a *thing*. But Lester was furious with himself for not seeing you home personally.
> (*to Clara Thornhill*)

Let's see. You must be Roger's mother. I'm so delighted to meet you. Roger's told us so much about you.
> (*to Larrabee*)

And you must be a policeman. You *look* like a policeman.

LARRABEE
I am Mr Thornhill's attorney.

THORNHILL
I want everybody here to know that I never even *saw* this woman before last night!

The Woman laughs good-naturedly at 'Roger's charming joke'. The detectives step forward.

CAPTAIN JUNKET
Mrs Townsend – I'm Captain Junket of the Nassau County Detectives, and this is Lieutenant Harding.

                          WOMAN
How do you do?

                        LT. HARDING
Ma'am.

                          WOMAN
                       (to Thornhill)
Oh, dear. You haven't gotten into trouble, Roger . . .?

    MRS THORNHILL   THORNHILL
     (simultaneously)   (simultaneously)
Has *he* gotten into *trouble*.   Stop calling me 'Roger'.

                      CAPTAIN JUNKET
Mrs Townsend – Mr Thornhill was picked up last night
driving while under the influence of alcohol, and incidentally,
in a stolen car –

                          WOMAN
Stolen car?

                      CAPTAIN JUNKET
– belonging to a Mrs Babson of Twining Road –

                          WOMAN
Roger, you said you were going to call a cab. You *didn't*
borrow Laura's Mercedes?

                        THORNHILL
                        (hopelessly)
No, I *didn't . . . borrow . . . Laura's . . . Mercedes.*

                      CAPTAIN JUNKET
Mr Thornhill has told us that he was brought to this house
against his will last night and forcibly intoxicated by some
friends of your husband and then set out on the road. Did
you know anything about this?

*The Woman gives Thornhill a look of deep sympathy, then faces the
detectives.*

                          WOMAN
Well, now, Captain – Roger *was* a bit tipsy when he arrived
here by cab for dinner –

                            41

THORNHILL

She's lying!

WOMAN

– And I'm afraid he became even worse as the evening wore on, and finally he told us he had to go home to sleep it off. I *knew* I should have served dinner earlier. Otherwise I can assure you the harmless little escapade with Mrs Babson's car would never have happened.

THORNHILL
(*with sardonic admiration*)

What a performance!

WOMAN

Poor dear . . .

CAPTAIN JUNKET

Mrs Townsend – does the name George Kaplan mean anything to you?

WOMAN
(*blankly*)

George Kaplan? No.

CAPTAIN JUNKET

I didn't think so.

The detective already has his eye on the door and a quick departure.

THORNHILL
(*desperate now*)

What about her husband? He's the one you should be questioning!

CAPTAIN JUNKET
(*to the Woman*)

Is there any place he can be reached?

WOMAN

Why yes – the United Nations.

                         CAPTAIN JUNKET
                           (*impressed*)
The . . . United . . . Nations . . .?

                              WOMAN
He's addressing the General Assembly this afternoon.

The detective looks at Thornhill and his mouth tightens.

                            THORNHILL
                            (*at bay*)
All right – so he's addressing the General Assembly.

                         CAPTAIN JUNKET
                         (*to the Woman*)
Sorry we had to bother you.

                              WOMAN
No bother at all.

She leads the group towards the door.

                            THORNHILL
Wait a minute now . . .

They go out to the foyer.

INT. THE FOYER

*As Thornhill is hurried by his mother out of the library across the foyer,
he hears:*

                         WOMAN'S VOICE
Will you be wanting to get in touch with my husband,
Captain?

                         CAPTAIN JUNKET
No, Mrs Townsend – that won't be necessary.

                            THORNHILL
D'you mean to say you're not going to do anything more
about this?

                    MRS THORNHILL
               (*turns, fixes him with a look*)
     Roger . . .
                    (*she shakes her head slowly*)
     Pay the two dollars.

*Thornhill gives her a look, then goes out the front door with her and the
others.*

EXT. MAIN HOUSE

*As the group goes down the steps and into the car, the Woman stands at
the door watching. She even waves once to Thornhill, who is in no
mood to wave back. On the lawn near the entrance, a gardener in
overalls is on his knees working over a flower bed. His back is to the
entrance, and he does not turn to see the group leave the house. But
now, as the car drives off, he gets to his feet, looks after the car, then
turns into camera. Beneath the overalls and the dirty face, we see
Valerian.*

     DISSOLVE TO:

EXT. PLAZA HOTEL. NEW YORK CITY – A FEW HOURS LATER

*A cab pulls up before the hotel. Thornhill and his mother get out and
cross the sidewalk to the entrance as:*

                    MRS THORNHILL
     I don't see what you need *me* along for.

                    THORNHILL
                    (*savagely*)
     You lend me a certain air of respectability.

                    MRS THORNHILL
     Don't be sarcastic, Roger.

They enter the hotel.

INT. LOBBY

Thornhill goes to the row of house phones, saying:

THORNHILL

Well, here goes.
(*he picks up a phone*)
Do you have a George Kaplan staying here?
(*a pause – then excitedly*)
That's right. Room seven ninety-six. Would you ring him
please?
(*to his mother*)
It's true. He *is* registered here . . .

MRS THORNHILL
(*bored*)

That's nice.

THORNHILL

. . . And he's just the one to clear up this little ballet.
(*to phone*)
What? . . . Oh. I see. He didn't leave any word when he'd be
back, did he? . . . Really? All right. Thank you.
(*he hangs up*)
That's funny. He hasn't answered his phone in two days.

MRS THORNHILL

Maybe he got locked in the bathroom.

*Thornhill has been peering thoughtfully towards the desk, where people
are getting their keys, mail, etc.*

THORNHILL

Mother – I want you to go over to the desk, put on that sweet
innocent look you do so well, and ask for the key to seven
ninety-six.

MRS THORNHILL

Don't be ridiculous. I wouldn't do a thing like that.

THORNHILL
(*taking out a wad of bills*)

Ten dollars?

MRS THORNHILL

Not for all the money in the world.

45

THORNHILL

Fifty?

MRS THORNHILL
(*taking the proffered money*)
You're disgraceful.

She starts towards the desk as Thornhill watches.

DISSOLVE TO:

INT. HOTEL CORRIDOR

Thornhill and his mother are walking towards the door to 796.

MRS THORNHILL
Car theft . . . drunk driving . . . assaulting an officer . . . lying
to a judge . . . and now, house-breaking . . .

THORNHILL
Not house-breaking, Mother. Hotel-breaking. There's a
difference.

MRS THORNHILL
(*gloomily*)
Of five to ten years.

*They arrive at 796; he takes the key from her hand and looks about
furtively. Then he inserts it in the lock. Just then, a chambermaid
emerges from another room, sees him and calls out:*

MAID
Just a minute please!

*Thornhill nervously pulls the key from the lock, turns and waits tensely
as she walks over to him.*

Will you be wantin' me to change your beddin', sir?

THORNHILL
(*relieved*)
Well . . . yes . . . but not right now . . .

MAID
I was only askin', sir, because the bed don't seem like it been

slept in and I was just wonderin' if I still oughta keep changin'
the linens, y'know?

> THORNHILL

Thank you very much for your interest.

> MAID
> (*smiling*)

You're welcome, sir.

*She goes off down the corridor. Quickly Thornhill inserts the key in the
lock, opens the door and leads his mother into the room.*

INT. HOTEL ROOM

> THORNHILL

You see that? She thought I was Kaplan. I wonder if I *look*
like Kaplan.

*He glances about. There are twin beds, neatly made up, but the rest of
the room looks lived-in. There is an open suitcase on the floor with a few
shirts and some soiled socks in it. On a chair is a three-day stack of
well-read New York newspapers. The dresser top is strewn with
masculine odds and ends – an electric shaver, a pair of military brushes
monogrammed 'G.K.', a half-empty pint of Canadian Club, several
scribbled reminders: 'Call Wilson', 'Laundry Friday', 'Wire
Ambassador East confirming reservation', 'Mahdi of Pakistan'. Also,
there is a group picture torn from a newspaper. The caption is missing,
but one of the faces has been ringed with red pencil. It is the face of the
Man of Glen Cove.*

> THORNHILL

Hmmm. Look who's here.

> MRS THORNHILL
> (*glancing about*)

Where? Who?

> THORNHILL

Our friend who's assembling the General Assembly this
afternoon.

He puts the picture down.

> MRS THORNHILL
>
> Roger – I think we should go.

As he goes to the night-table and presses a button marked 'Chambermaid':

> THORNHILL
>
> Don't be nervous, Mother.

> MRS THORNHILL
>
> I'm not nervous. I'll be late for the bridge club.

> THORNHILL
>
> Good. You'll lose less than usual.

He goes to the bathroom and enters.

INT. THE BATHROOM

There are toilet articles on the sink, on the glass shelf above it, and in the medicine cabinet. Thornhill takes the comb from the hairbrush on the shelf, inspects it, then replaces it. He returns to:

INT. THE BEDROOM

> THORNHILL
>
> Bulletin. Mr Kaplan has dandruff.

> MRS THORNHILL
>
> In that case, I think we'd better leave.

Just then, the door buzzer sounds.

> Too late.

Thornhill goes to the door, opens it. The Chambermaid stands there.

> MAID
>
> You rang for me?

> THORNHILL
>
> Come in a moment.
> > (*the Maid enters*)
>
> What's your name?

48

MAID

Elsie, sir.

THORNHILL

Elsie – do you know who I am?

MAID
(*giggles*)

Sure. You're Mr Kaplan.

THORNHILL

When did we . . . when did you first see me, Elsie?

MAID

Outside the door, out there in the hall, just a couple minutes
ago. Don'tcha remember?

THORNHILL

You mean that's the first time you ever laid eyes on me?

MAID

Can I help it you're never *around*, Mr Kaplan?

THORNHILL

How do you know I *am* Mr Kaplan?

MAID
(*puzzled*)

Huh?

THORNHILL

How do you know I'm Mr Kaplan?

MAID
(*giggles*)

Well, of *course* ya are. This is room seven ninety-six, isn't it?
So – you're the gentleman in room seven ninety-six, aren't
ya?

THORNHILL

All right, Elsie.

MAID

Will that be all, sir?

49

THORNHILL

For the time being. Yes.

*As the Maid starts away, the door buzzer sounds again. The Maid
opens the door and goes out past the Valet, who is seen standing there
with a suit on a hanger.*

VALET

Valet.

THORNHILL

Come in.

VALET
(entering)

Hang it in the closet, Mr Kaplan?

THORNHILL

Please.

*Thornhill exchanges a look with his mother as the Valet opens the closet
door, hangs the suit on the rack.*

VALET

There we are.
(Thornhill gives him a tip)
Thank you, Mr Kaplan.

THORNHILL

By the way – when did I give you that suit?

VALET

Last night. Around six.

THORNHILL

Did I give it to you personally?

VALET
(smiles)

Personally? No, Mr Kaplan. You called down on the phone
and described the suit to me and said it would be hanging in
the closet. Like you always do. Anything wrong?

THORNHILL

No, no. Just curious.

VALET
(*leaving*)
Okay. Nice meeting you, Mr Kaplan.

He goes out. Thornhill steps to the closet, opens the door.

THORNHILL
I'm beginning to think nobody in this hotel has actually ever *seen* Kaplan.

MRS THORNHILL
Maybe he has his suits mended by Invisible Weavers.

There are several suits on the rack. Thornhill takes one out, tosses it on a chair, whips off his jacket, throws it on the bed, then takes the other jacket off the hanger and puts it on. He extends his arms. The sleeves are eight inches too short.

(*looking him over speculatively*)
I don't think that one *does* anything for you.

Thornhill takes the trousers from the hanger, holds them up in front of him. They are ludicrously short.

THORNHILL

Look at this. They've mistaken me for a man who is only five feet tall.

MRS THORNHILL

I've always *told* you to stand up straight.

Just then, the telephone on the night-table rings. Thornhill stares at it uncertainly. The phone rings again.

THORNHILL

Should I?

MRS THORNHILL

Certainly not.

So Thornhill goes over and picks up the receiver.

THORNHILL

Hello?

VALERIAN'S VOICE
(*through phone*)

It is good to find you in, Mr Kaplan.

THORNHILL

Who is this?

VALERIAN'S VOICE
(*through phone*)

We met only last night and still you do not recognize my voice. I should feel offended –

THORNHILL

Yeah – now I know who you are and I'm *not* Mr Kaplan.

VALERIAN'S VOICE
(*through phone*)

Of course not. You answer his telephone and you live in his hotel room, and yet you are not Mr Kaplan. Nevertheless, we are pleased to find you in.

He clicks off.

THORNHILL

Hello?
(*jiggling receiver frantically*)
Hello!

OPERATOR'S VOICE
(*through phone*)
Yes?

THORNHILL
Operator, this is Mr Thorn – Mr Kaplan in seven ninety-six.
That call that just came through. Was that an *outside* call or
from the lobby?

OPERATOR'S VOICE
(*through phone*)
Just a minute, sir. I'll see.

THORNHILL
Hurry!

MRS THORNHILL
Who was it?

THORNHILL
Only one of the men who tried to kill me last night.

MRS THORNHILL
Oh – we're back to *that* one, are we?

THORNHILL
(*jiggling the phone*)
Hello – *operator*!

OPERATOR'S VOICE
(*through phone*)
Mr Kaplan . . .

THORNHILL
Yes . . .

OPERATOR'S VOICE
(*through phone*)
That call was made from the lobby, sir.

53

It was . . .

(*he hangs up, looks about desperately*)
The lobby. They're probably on their way up right now.
Come on. We've got to get out of here.

He struggles into his jacket, picks up the newspaper clipping and stuffs it in his pocket.

MRS THORNHILL
(*not at all excited*)
I think I'd like to *meet* one of these killers.

He takes her by the arm, hurries her to the door.

INT. THE CORRIDOR

As they emerge from the room, Thornhill looks about, sees no one, moves his mother swiftly to the nearby elevator. He presses the 'DOWN' button, waits anxiously. Suddenly two elevators arrive simultaneously, one from above, the other from below. Just as Thornhill and his mother enter their elevator, Valerian and Licht step out of the other one, in time to see their quarry. Before the doors can close, they quickly follow Thornhill in.

INT. ELEVATOR

There are six passengers in the car, all of them of obvious refinement and sophistication: an elderly gentleman and his elderly wife; two fiftyish women; and another couple. Valerian and Licht are crowded close to Thornhill and his mother as the doors close and the elevator starts down. Thornhill taps her and indicates that these are the men who are after him. She glances at them and sees two men whose attitude seems to be quite innocuous. She turns back to Thornhill and smiles her disbelief. He frowns and nods his insistence. She turns to them again and smiles.

MRS THORNHILL
You gentleman aren't *really* trying to kill my son, are you?

The men look at her blankly, as the other passengers turn their heads in surprise. Valerian starts to smile, as he turns to Licht, who takes the cue

54

and also begins to smile. *Valerian turns towards the other occupants of the car and starts to chuckle. Relieved, they start to chuckle too. For a split second, Mrs Thornhill is astonished at the effect of her remark. Then she too joins in the laughter. By now the laughter has built to a crescendo and the whole car is laughing, even the operator. In the center of all this stands a glowering Thornhill. The elevator comes to a stop.*

OPERATOR

Lobby, please. Watch your step.

Thornhill's expression immediately changes to one of furtive calculation. We hear the sound of the elevator door opening and the outside lobby lights appear on his face. Valerian and Licht start to move out.

THORNHILL
(to both of them, politely)

Excuse me. Ladies first, if you don't mind.

INT. LOBBY

Camera is shooting into the elevator. Thornhill turns and starts backing out of the car as he ushers the ladies out. The ladies, in pushing their way out, ease Valerian and Licht towards the rear. As Thornhill backs away, the camera also retreats with him, but goes faster than he does. Thornhill is now far enough out to turn towards the camera and start running towards the 59th Street entrance, the camera panning with him.

INT. LOBBY – ANOTHER ANGLE

Thornhill is now running towards the camera. Behind him we see Valerian and Licht pushing their way between the women, and just in front of them, Mrs Thornhill, who is calling out:

MRS THORNHILL

Roger – will you be home for dinner?

Thornhill dashes out of the shot.

EXT. PLAZA HOTEL

A man and woman are waiting for a taxi, which is just pulling up. As the doorman opens the door for them, Thornhill comes dashing out of the

*hotel, runs down the steps and jumps into the cab, past the astonished
people. He slams the door shut and the cab starts to move off.*

INT. CAB

                            DRIVER
Where to?

                            THORNHILL
I don't know. Just keep going.

*The Driver shrugs. Thornhill turns, looks out of the back window. Over
his shoulder we see Valerian and Licht dashing across the sidewalk and
past the same startled couple and doorman into the next cab, which has
just pulled up. Thornhill turns away, realizing he is still being followed,
ponders the situation, then reaches into his pocket, takes out the torn
newspaper photograph he had found in the hotel room and glances down
at it thoughtfully. He looks up at the cab-driver.*

                            THORNHILL
Take me to the United Nations.

                            DRIVER
Right.

                            THORNHILL
The General Assembly Building.

                            DRIVER
Right.

                            THORNHILL
I'm being followed. Can you do something about it?

                            DRIVER
Yes. I can.

                            THORNHILL
Do it.

The cab surges forward with a burst of speed.

DISSOLVE TO:

EXT. UNITED NATIONS HEADQUARTERS – DAY

As seen from the north, a long high-angle shot showing the General Assembly building in the foreground, the 39-story marble and glass Secretariat building beyond it and, in the background, the East River and the Brooklyn skyline. At the extreme right, a taxicab is seen pulling up at the curb near the main entrance to the General Assembly building.

ENTRANCE. GENERAL ASSEMBLY BUILDING

CLOSE ANGLE: *Thornhill gets out of the cab, goes into the building.*

INT. LOBBY. GENERAL ASSEMBLY BUILDING

Thornhill crosses to the information desk. There are two girls stationed behind the desk, one of them a lovely Indian. She smiles at Thornhill.

GIRL

May I help you, sir?

THORNHILL

Yes. Where would I find Mr Lester Townsend?

GIRL
(writing on a pad)

Mr Townsend of UNIPO. And did you have an appointment, sir?

THORNHILL

I . . . uh . . . yes . . . uh . . . he expects me,

GIRL

Your name, sir?

THORNHILL
(hesitates)

My name?

GIRL

Yes, please.

THORNHILL

Kaplan. George Kaplan.

One moment, please.

She picks up a phone, starts to dial. Thornhill glances back towards the entrance door nervously.

EXT. STREET NEAR MAIN ENTRANCE

Another cab is seen pulling up to the curb. Valerian gets out and, addressing Licht inside, gestures as though telling him to have the cab wait across the street. As the cab pulls away Valerian starts up the steps to the main entrance of the General Assembly building.

INT. LOBBY

Thornhill is now receiving a slip of paper from the Girl at the information desk, who is saying:

GIRL
. . . If you will give this to one of the attendants in the Public Lounge she will page him for you.

THORNHILL
Thank you very much.

GIRL
You're welcome, Mr Kaplan.

Thornhill starts past the desk.

EXT. MAIN ENTRANCE

Valerian crosses the courtyard and starts through the main doors.

INT. LOBBY

Valerian enters and glances about. Then he walks in the direction of the information desk.

INT. PUBLIC LOUNGE

Thornhill is just approaching the lounge. We enter with him, see the vast, high-ceilinged room with its high windows along the north wall looking out on the East River and the Queensboro Bridge in the distance. *The lounge is crowded with delegates of all nations; there are many races, many different modes of dress. They sit on leather chairs and sofas sipping tea, or stand in small conversational groups with cocktails in hand. Others congregate at the bar at the east end of the room. Everywhere is the buzz of many different tongues. And over it, the Continuing Sound of the Public Address System as three pretty attendants seated behind microphones near the telephone switchboard send out their calls:*

VOICES OVER PA SYSTEM
'Miss Knox of Ceylon . . . United States Secretary please . . . Mr Mahdi, delegation of Pakistan, please call the Public Lounge . . . Mr Craig of the Secretariat, kindly call your office . . . Mr Bernatti of the Swiss Observers Office . . . Mr Bernatti of the Swiss Observers Office . . .'

Thornhill goes up to one of the attendants (a 26-year-old American girl), hands her the slip of paper.

THORNHILL
Will you page Mr Lester Townsend, please?

ATTENDANT
(*consulting the slip*)
Certainly, Mr Kaplan.

She picks up the microphone. We hear her voice over the PA system.

Mr Townsend of UNIPO . . . Mr Townsend of UNIPO . . . Please call at the communications desk of the Public Lounge.

Thornhill stands gazing about the crowded room waiting for Townsend to appear. Deep in background we see Valerian enter. He stops as he sees Thornhill. There is a constant stream of activity at the communications desk. Several different people emerge from the throng to walk over to the desk. Thornhill pays them no attention, for none of them is the man he is seeking. Finally one caller – a distinguished-looking gentleman of about sixty – leans over and speaks to the attendant, who then glances at Thornhill.

ATTENDANT
Mr Kaplan . . .

                    THORNHILL
                    (*turning*)
Yes?

                    ATTENDANT
You wished to see Mr Townsend.

                    THORNHILL
Yes.

                    ATTENDANT
                    (*pointing*)
This is Mr Townsend.

Thornhill looks at the strange man, blinks with puzzlement.

                    TOWNSEND
How do you do, Mr Kaplan?

He extends his hand.

                    THORNHILL
                    (*to attendant*)
This isn't Mr Townsend.

                    TOWNSEND
                    (*smiling*)
Yes it is.

He holds out his hand again. Thornhill shakes it dumbly.

                    THORNHILL
There must be . . . some . . . mistake. *Lester* Townsend?

                    TOWNSEND
                    (*cheerfully*)
That's me.
                    (*as they stroll towards the windows*)
What can I do for you?

                    THORNHILL
                    (*still utterly bewildered*)
You're the Townsend who lives in Glen Cove?

                    TOWNSEND
That's right. Are we neighbors?

THORNHILL
A large red-brick house with a curving tree-lined driveway?

TOWNSEND
(*smiles*)
That's the one.

As they walk across the room, they pass a press photographer taking flashbulb shots of a West African group.

THORNHILL
Mr Townsend, were you at home last night?

TOWNSEND
You mean in Glen Cove?

THORNHILL
Yes.

TOWNSEND
No. I've been staying in my apartment in town for the past month. Always do when we're in session here.

THORNHILL
What about *Mrs* Townsend?

TOWNSEND
(*frowns*)
My wife has been dead for many years.
(*Thornhill stares at him*)
Look here, Mr Kaplan, what's this all about?

THORNHILL
Who are those people living in your house?

TOWNSEND
What people? The house is completely closed up. There's just a gardener and his wife living on the grounds. Now, Mr Kaplan – suppose you tell me who you are and what you want.

Thornhill takes the newspaper photograph from his pocket, starts to show it to Townsend.

THORNHILL

Do you know this man?

*Townsend glances at the picture, then suddenly gasps and utters a
strangled cry. His eyes widen and he sags against Thornhill, who puts
his arms around him automatically to support him.*

Here. What's wrong?

*Townsend groans. His eyes flutter. Thornhill's right hand closes on the
handle of a knife protruding from Townsend's back. Instinctively, he
grasps the knife, pulls it out. Townsend slumps to the floor, dead.
Thornhill stands there in horror staring down at him, the bloody knife in
his upraised hand. It has all happened so swiftly that nobody has
actually seen the slaying. Valerian is seen hurrying away. A woman's
voice is heard crying out: 'Look!' A man's voice shouts: 'What
happened?' Thornhill looks up, sees a circle of horrified, angry faces
staring at him. A woman points at him accusingly: 'He did it! I saw
him!' The group moves towards him slowly, threateningly. Another
voice cries out: 'Look out! He's got a knife!' Thornhill backs away
slowly, dazed and confused.*

Wait a minute now . . . Listen to me . . . I had nothing to do
with this . . .

VOICES
(*overlapping*)
Somebody do something! . . . I saw him! . . . Call the police!
. . . Grab him! . . .

THORNHILL
(*frightened*)
Don't come any nearer! Get back!

*There is a click and a flash of light. The press photographer has
whipped his camera around and caught a perfect shot of the stunned
Thornhill backing away from the fallen body with the bloody knife still
clenched threateningly in his hand. Panic on his face, he drops the knife
and flees from the room before the startled onlookers can make a move.*

DISSOLVE TO:

62

INT. CONFERENCE ROOM. CENTRAL INTELLIGENCE AGENCY.
WASHINGTON, DC – EARLY EVENING

Start close on front page of a Washington evening paper featuring the incriminating photo of Thornhill in his 'killer's' pose; above it, screamer headlines: 'DIPLOMAT SLAIN AT UN; ASSASSIN ELUDES POLICE'. *A man's voice is heard over the shot reading aloud what is obviously part of the news story. During this we pull back to reveal a group of four men and one woman seated around a conference table. As the camera leaves the insert of the newspaper and starts its rise, we also catch a glimpse of official documents on which we see the words:* 'TOP SECRET'.

> MAN'S VOICE
> (*reading*)
> . . . The photograph has been tentatively identified as that of Roger Thornhill, a Manhattan advertising executive, indicating that the name George Kaplan, which he gave to an attendant in the General Assembly Building, was false. A possible motive for the slaying was suggested by the discovery that earlier today, Thornhill appeared in a Glen Cove, Long Island, police court on a charge of drunk driving with a stolen

car, and in his defense charged that the murder victim, Mr Townsend, had attempted to kill *him* the night before . . .

The man puts the newspaper down on the table, looks up at the other people. Their ages vary from thirty-five to fifty; there is nothing about an Intelligence agent's appearance that distinguishes them from, say, a college professor or a stockbroker or a reporter or a housewife. These people happen to be all of that, too. The gentleman who has been reading the newspaper, for example, is, among other things, a limner of comic cartoons for the national magazines.

CARTOONIST

Brother . . .

STOCKBROKER

What about that?

HOUSEWIFE

Does anybody *know* this Thornhill?

CARTOONIST

Not me.

STOCKBROKER

Never heard of him.

HOUSEWIFE

Professor?

The Professor shakes his head negatively.

REPORTER

Apparently the poor sucker got mistaken for George Kaplan.

CARTOONIST

How could he be mistaken for George Kaplan when George Kaplan doesn't even exist?

REPORTER

Don't ask me how it happened, but obviously it happened. Vandamm's men must have grabbed him and tried to put him away, using Lester Townsend's house.

STOCKBROKER
(*nodding*)
And the unsuspecting Townsend winds up with a stray knife
in his back.

REPORTER
(*shrugs*)
C'est la guerre.

CARTOONIST
(*shaking his head*)
It's so horribly sad. Why is it I feel like laughing?

HOUSEWIFE
Never mind *that*. What are we going to do?

CARTOONIST
Do?

HOUSEWIFE
About Mr Thornhill . . .

STOCKBROKER
Good question.

*They look at each other uncertainly. Finally the mildest mannered of
them all, the College Professor, speaks up quietly, enunciating with
elaborate preciseness.*

PROFESSOR
We do . . . nothing.

HOUSEWIFE
Nothing?

PROFESSOR
(*getting up*)
That's right . . . nothing.
(*with a gesture*)
Oh, we *could* congratulate ourselves on a marvelous stroke of
good fortune . . .
(*he meets their puzzled stares with a delighted announcement*)
Our non-existent decoy, George Kaplan – created to divert

suspicion from our own Number One – has fortuitously become a *live* decoy.

HOUSEWIFE

Yes, Professor. And how long do you think he's going to *stay* live?

PROFESSOR

That's *his* problem.

STOCKBROKER

What Mrs Finley means –

PROFESSOR
(*amused*)

I know what she means.

STOCKBROKER

– We can't just sit back calmly and wait to see who kills him first . . . Vandamm and company or the police.

PROFESSOR
(*forcefully*)

There's nothing we can do to save him without endangering Number One!

HOUSEWIFE

Aren't we being just a wee bit callous?

The Professor's tolerant attitude vanishes.

PROFESSOR

No, my dear woman, we are *not* being callous. We did not invent our non-existent man, and establish elaborate behaviour patterns for him, and move his prop belongings in and out of hotel rooms, for our *own private amusement*. We created George Kaplan and labored to convince Vandamm that this phantom was our own Number One, hot on his trail, for a *desperately important reason*.

REPORTER

Check.

STOCKBROKER
Nobody's denying that.

PROFESSOR
(*passionately*)
All right then. If we make the slightest move to suggest that
there *is* no such agent as George Kaplan . . . give *any* hint to
Vandamm that he's pursuing a *decoy* instead of our real
Number One . . . then Number One, working right under
Vandamm's nose, will immediately face suspicion, exposure
and assassination, like the two others who went before.

*There is a moment of embarrassed silence around the table as they all
realize the unpleasant truth of what the Professor has just said.*

HOUSEWIFE
(*softly, sadly*)
Goodbye, Mr Thornhill . . . wherever you are.

DISSOLVE TO:

INT. GRAND CENTRAL STATION. NYC – EARLY EVENING

*Shooting from a high vantage point, we disclose the vast, bustling main
lobby of the terminal. Police are seen entering from the 42nd Street side –
two lieutenants in uniform and two plain-clothes detectives. They look
about, come to a stop, confer and then disperse. Camera pans slightly to
a phone booth. We see Thornhill inside, talking on the phone.*

INT. PHONE BOOTH

THORNHILL
(*exasperated*)
But, Mother, I *called* the Plaza. Kaplan checked out and went
to the Ambassador East in Chicago. That's why I'm –
(*he listens impatiently*)
I *can't* go to the police. Not yet. *You* saw the newspapers. My
fingerprints are on the knife; I'm a drunk driver, a car thief
and I murdered a man for revenge. I wouldn't have a chance,
and I *won't* have until I find George Kaplan, who obviously
knows what this is all about.
(*listens again*)

No, the train. It's safer.
> (*another interruption*)

Because there's no room to hide on a plane if someone
should recognize me. You want me to jump off a moving
plane?
> (*nods, then with angry sarcasm*)

Thank you so much, Mother.

*There is a loud clatter as Mrs Thornhill hangs up on him. Thornhill
stares at the receiver a moment, then hangs up and pushes out of the
booth.*

INT. TERMINAL

*As he emerges from the booth, he comes face to face with a large man
who could be a detective. For a brief, tense moment they stare at each
other, and then the man steps past him into the booth. Thornhill looks
about cautiously, then starts walking across the lobby towards the ticket
windows, camera moving with him. Near the information booth, a man
stands reading the center pages of the* NY Post. *Thornhill sees the front
page headlines:* 'MANHUNT ON FOR UN KILLER'. *This reminds him to
take out dark glasses and put them on, which he does as he continues
across the lobby and steps up to a Pullman ticket window. A Ticket
Agent moves up to him, peers at the dark glasses.*

AGENT

Yes?

THORNHILL

Give me a bedroom or whatever you got on the Twentieth
Century.

AGENT
(slowly)

Leaving in five minutes.

THORNHILL
(impatiently)

I know. Come on.

AGENT

I think they're all sold out.

                    THORNHILL
Sold out?

                    AGENT
You can always go coach.

                    THORNHILL
No, I . . . I can't. When's the next train?

                    AGENT
Nothing till ten.
                (*peering at him*)
You're in a hurry, huh?

                    THORNHILL
                (*sharply*)
Call them and see what you can do.

                    AGENT
                (*still peering*)
Something wrong with your eyes?

                    THORNHILL
Yes. They're sensitive to questions. Will you *call* them?

                    AGENT
                (*still staring at him*)
Sure . . . sure . . .

REVERSE ANGLE: TICKET OFFICE
*We are behind the agent, shooting through the window opening on
Thornhill. What we see (and Thornhill cannot) is that the agent is now
looking down at a glossy photograph of Thornhill with knife in hand,
obviously a police department copy of the original. He glances up at
Thornhill again.*

                    AGENT
Don't go away.

*The agent walks away from the window, camera moving with him. Out
of Thornhill's line of sight in the rear of the ticket office, he picks up a
phone, dials three times, waits, then –*
                (*softly, into phone*)

                        69

He's at Window Fifteen, upper-level. Hurry.

He hangs up, swallows nervously, composes himself, steps to the ticket rack, takes down a ticket, returns to the window saying airily:

You're in luck, mister –

He stops, stares. Nobody is at the window. He leans through, peers about. Thornhill is gone.

LONG SHOT: THE TERMINAL
Thornhill has withdrawn to a vantage point across the lobby. In distant background the agent is seen pulling his head back in. In close foreground, Thornhill stands watching him, hidden by the intervening crowds. Now he sees two men – the police lieutenants – hurrying up to the ticket window, conferring with the agent, then turning, looking about.

ANOTHER ANGLE
Thornhill turns away, moves swiftly towards the train platform entrances, camera dollying with him. He sees the sign above Track 29: TWENTIETH CENTURY LIMITED. *He starts through the gate. A Guard stops him.*

GUARD

Ticket?

THORNHILL
I . . . uh . . . I'm just seeing some friends off.

He starts through. The Guard grabs him.

GUARD
Sorry. I'll have to know their name and space before I can let you through.

Thornhill looks back, sees the police running across the lobby towards the gate. He yanks his arm free, pushes the Guard aside, goes through the gate and runs past the desk where train officials are verifying passenger space.

EXT. THE PLATFORM

> GUARD'S VOICE
> (*off-screen*)

Wait a minute! Come back here!

Thornhill continues to run, camera moving with him. In background, the police reach the gate, confer with the Guard. As Thornhill reaches the rear car of the waiting train, he turns, looks back. The police are coming after him. Up and down the platform, porters are calling out: 'All Aboard!' Thornhill quickly boards the train.

INT. TRAIN

Thornhill hurries through a car, looks out of the window, takes his dark glasses off and sees the police running along the platform to enter the car up ahead. He turns, starts back. Another passenger is approaching. It is a lovely, smartly-dressed Girl of twenty-six. Thornhill tries to get past her. The aisle is narrow. She steps to one side. But he steps to the same side. He moves to the other side – just as she does.

> GIRL

Sorry.

> THORNHILL

My fault.

They move to the center – but in unison. Again an impasse.

Sorry.

> GIRL

My fault.

Meanwhile, the police have boarded the train. Thornhill and the girl are getting nowhere, just blocking each other. The police come into view at the other end of the car. Momentarily distracted by an outgoing Redcap, they haven't spotted Thornhill yet. The Girl sees the men, notices their uniforms, senses Thornhill's urgency. Thornhill catches her look, ducks into an open compartment filled with luggage but no passenger as yet, and pulls the door partially closed. The police come running through the car.

GIRL
(*pointing*)
He went that way. I think he got off.

They follow her directions, continue on. The compartment door opens, Thornhill steps out, sees the coast is clear.

THORNHILL
Thank you very much.

GIRL
Quite all right.

THORNHILL
(*lamely*)
Seven parking tickets.

GIRL
Oh.

She walks away. He looks after her. The view is quite attractive. The train starts moving. He peers out of the window.

EXT. THE PLATFORM

The police have been searching the platform. They turn, watch helplessly as the train pulls away.

DISSOLVE TO:

EXT. NY CENTRAL TRACKS – NIGHT

Somewhere along the Hudson River, the Twentieth Century Limited comes around a bend, speeds towards camera and races by.

INT. CLUB CAR

A Pullman Conductor and his assistant are finishing up the business of collecting tickets and verifying Pullman space. They move through the car, studying the passengers who sit there reading magazines and newspapers, recognizing most of them as having handed over their tickets earlier. There is doubt about one passenger, an elderly woman.

Do I have your ticket, madam?

Why yes. I gave it to you an hour ago.

And that space was . . . ?

Bedroom F. in Car eighteen-oh-one.

(consulting his chart)
Thank you.

(a little huffy)
You're welcome.

The Conductor and his Assistant continue on until they come to a door labelled: 'WASHROOM'. The Assistant tries the handle, finds the door unlocked, opens it slightly and peers in. Satisfied that the washroom is unoccupied, he closes the door, and the two men continue on.

After a moment, the washroom door opens, Thornhill peers out, then emerges and moves off in the opposite direction through the club car. As he passes a table, he sees an evening paper lying there with his own picture on the front page, face up. He stops, casually turns the paper over, and continues on towards the dining car.

INT. DINING CAR

As Thornhill enters from the next car, the Steward approaches him.

Good evening, sir. One?

Please.

The Steward leads him into the dining area. It is fairly crowded. The Girl is there, seated alone at a table for two. She is on dessert and coffee. Without a word, the Steward leads Thornhill directly to her table and

*pulls out the chair for him. The Girl looks up at Thornhill, smiles
fleetingly. He returns the smile and sits down.*

> STEWARD

Cocktail before dinner?

> THORNHILL

How about a Gibson?

> STEWARD

Right away.

*He goes off. Thornhill takes up the menu, studies it. The Girl raises her
eyes, studies him. He looks up, catches her glance. She quickly looks
down. He glances down at the menu again, then looks up at her. She
glances up, catches him, and he looks away. Now she looks away.
Then they both look up at each other at the same time and meet head
on. They smile.*

> THORNHILL

Well – here we are again.

> GIRL

Yes.

> THORNHILL
> *(looking down at menu)*

Recommend anything?

> GIRL

The brook trout. A little 'trouty' but quite good.

> THORNHILL

Sold.

*He writes out the order. A waiter brings his Gibson, takes the order and
leaves. Thornhill glances about the dining car nervously, sees (or
perhaps imagines he sees) several people staring at him. When he looks
back at the Girl, he finds that she is scrutinizing him.*

I know. I look vaguely familiar to you.

> GIRL

Yes.

74

THORNHILL

You feel you've seen me somewhere before.

GIRL

Yes.

THORNHILL

Funny how I have that effect on people wherever I go.
Something about my face . . .

GIRL

It's a nice face.

THORNHILL

You really think so?

GIRL

I would never say it if I didn't.

THORNHILL

Oh – you're *that* type.

GIRL

What type?

THORNHILL

Honest.

GIRL

Not really.

THORNHILL

Good. Honest women frighten me.

GIRL

Why?

THORNHILL

I feel at a disadvantage with them.

GIRL

Because *you're* not honest with *them*.

THORNHILL

Exactly.

75

GIRL

Like that business about the seven parking tickets . . .

THORNHILL
(*stepping delicately past it*)
What I mean is: the moment I meet an attractive girl, I have
to start pretending that I've no desire to make love to her.

GIRL
What makes you think you have to conceal it?

THORNHILL
She might find the idea objectionable.

GIRL
(*provocatively*)
And then again, she might not.

THORNHILL
Think how lucky I am to have been seated here.

GIRL
Luck had nothing to do with it.

THORNHILL
Fate?

GIRL
I tipped the steward five dollars to seat you here if you should
come in.

Thornhill looks at her for a long moment.

THORNHILL
Is that a proposition?

She looks right back at him for an equally long moment.

GIRL
I never make love on an empty stomach.

THORNHILL
You've already eaten.

GIRL
But you haven't.

They continue to gaze at each other, and then the waiter brings dinner and sets it on the table. Thornhill goes to work on it.

THORNHILL

Don't you think it's time we were introduced?

GIRL

I'm Eve Kendall. Twenty-six and unmarried. Now you know everything.

THORNHILL

What do you do besides lure men to their doom on the New York Central?

EVE

I'm an industrial designer.

THORNHILL

Jack Phillips. Western sales manager of Kingby Electronics.

EVE
(*easily*)

No you're not. You're Roger Thornhill of Madison Avenue and you're wanted for murder on every front page in America. Don't be so modest.

THORNHILL

Oops.

EVE

Don't worry. I won't say a word.

THORNHILL

How come?

EVE

I told you – it's a nice face.

THORNHILL

Is that the only reason?

EVE
(*shrugs*)

It's going to be a long night . . .

THORNHILL
(*nods*)

True.

EVE

And I don't particularly like the book I've started . . .

THORNHILL

Ah.

EVE

You know what I mean?

THORNHILL

Oh – exactly.

Eve puts a cigarette between her lips, looks quite boldly into Thornhill's eyes as he takes a folder of matches from his pocket. She notices the match folder, takes it from him and examines it. (We will see it in an insert.) On each side of the folder, three large letters: ROT.
(*explaining*)

My trademark – rot.

EVE

Roger O. Thornhill. What's the O. for?

THORNHILL

Nothing.

He strikes a match to light her cigarette. (Meanwhile, the train has been slowing down as it approaches a station.) She takes his hand in hers and guides the flame to her cigarette, her hands lingering on his with an unmistakable intimacy that he finds downright delightful.

I'd invite you to my bedroom if I had a bedroom.

EVE

Roomette?

THORNHILL

Nothing – not even a ticket. I've been playing hide-and-seek with the Pullman conductor ever since we left New York.

EVE

How awkward for you.

THORNHILL

No place to sleep.

EVE

I've got a large drawing-room all to myself.

THORNHILL

That's not fair, is it?

EVE

Drawing-room E, car thirty-nine-oh-one.

THORNHILL

A nice number.

EVE

Easy to remember.

THORNHILL

Thirty-nine-oh-one.

EVE

See?

THORNHILL

I have no luggage.

EVE
(*looking out of the window*)

So?

THORNHILL

You wouldn't happen to have an extra pair of pajamas, would you?

She looks him right in the eye.

EVE

Wouldn't I?

Then she puts money on her tab and gets to her feet, as Thornhill stares up at her, slightly awed. The train comes to a stop.

Incidentally, I wouldn't order any dessert if I were you.

THORNHILL
(*pats his stomach*)

I get the message.

EVE

That wasn't quite what I meant. The train seems to be making an unscheduled stop, and I just saw two men getting out of a police car as we pulled into the station. They weren't smiling.

She walks away, and Thornhill looks out of the window. Two Detectives are seen hurrying along the platform to board the train. Thornhill puts some money on the table, gets to his feet and saunters out of the car in the direction Eve has taken. Camera pans quickly to the other end of the car, picks up the two Detectives entering the dining area and looking about. The Steward walks up to them, as the train starts moving again.

DISSOLVE TO:

INT. EVE'S DRAWING-ROOM — LATER

Eve is seated by the window with a book in her lap, apparently alone. Thornhill is nowhere to be seen. Sometime during the scene, the camera will indicate to us that his muffled voice is coming from behind the closed upper berth, where he is locked in. Eve continues to glance at her book as she speaks.

THORNHILL'S VOICE
I think you better go out and tell those police to hurry.

EVE
Patience is a virtue.

THORNHILL'S VOICE
So is breathing.

EVE
Just lie still.

THORNHILL'S VOICE
Do you have any olive oil?

EVE
Olive oil?

THORNHILL'S VOICE
I want to be packed in olive oil if I'm going to be a sardine.

The door buzzer sounds. Eve remains seated, calls out in a loud voice:

EVE
Come in.

The door opens. The dining-car Steward is seen in the corridor. He looks in at Eve, speaks apologetically.

STEWARD
I'm sorry to disturb you. Some gentlemen here would like to have a word with you.

MAN'S VOICE
(*off-screen*)
Okay. Thanks.

The Steward goes off, and the two Detectives enter.

81

FIRST DETECTIVE
Your name, please?

EVE
Eve Kendall. Who are you?

FIRST DETECTIVE
(*showing identification*)
State Police.

EVE
Is anything wrong?

Meanwhile, the Second Detective is opening the closet door and the lavatory door and peering into every nook and cranny of the drawing-room.

FIRST DETECTIVE
There was a man seated at your table tonight in the dining car.

EVE
Yes.

FIRST DETECTIVE
Friend of yours?

EVE
I never saw him before.

FIRST DETECTIVE
This the man?

He hands her a photograph. She takes it, studies it.

EVE
Why yes. I think so. It's not a very clear picture.

FIRST DETECTIVE
It's a wire photo. We just got it from the New York police.

EVE
Police?

FIRST DETECTIVE
He's wanted for murder.

EVE
(*getting up*)

Good heavens. No.

FIRST DETECTIVE

We thought maybe he was in here with you.

EVE

With me? I told you, I don't even know the man.

FIRST DETECTIVE

The steward said you left the dining car together.

EVE

We might have happened to *leave* at the same time but not together.

FIRST DETECTIVE

What did you two talk about?

EVE

Talk about?

FIRST DETECTIVE

Yeah. Your waiter said you were getting along pretty good with this Thornhill fellow.

EVE

Is that his name – Thornhill?

FIRST DETECTIVE

Didn't he tell you?

EVE

No. Didn't tell me anything. All we did was chat . . . about different kinds of food . . . train travel versus plane travel . . . that sort of thing . . . rather innocuous, I must say, considering that he was a fugitive from justice. Who did he kill?

FIRST DETECTIVE

He didn't say where he was going, did he?

EVE

No – I assumed Chicago. You think perhaps he got off when you got on?

83

FIRST DETECTIVE
(*rather grimly*)
Look - if you happen to catch sight of him again, Miss . . . uh –

EVE
Kendall.

FIRST DETECTIVE
. . . Will you let us know?

EVE
I'm going to bed soon, and I intend to lock my door, so I doubt if I'll be seeing him or anybody else tonight.

FIRST DETECTIVE
Well just in case you do – we'll be in the observation car at the rear of the train.

EVE
It's comforting to know that.

Disgruntled, the two men walk out.

Good night.

She closes the door, goes quickly to her handbag as she says:

Still breathing?

THORNHILL'S VOICE
(*pleading weakly*)
Either hurry, or bring me a snorkel.

EVE
(*fumbling in her bag*)
I'm looking for that can opener I stole from the porter.

She takes out the key-like device which porters use to open Pullman beds. She inserts it in the lock, turns it, and the upper berth crashes open, bouncing Thornhill into view.

Hello there.

He sits up, heaves a sigh of relief, removes his sun-glasses from his pocket and stares sourly at them. They are smashed. He drops the pieces on the bed, then looks down at Eve and smiles with friendly puzzlement.

(*during above*)
All clear.

THORNHILL

Why are you so good to me?

She gazes up at him and smiles.

EVE

Shall I climb up and tell you why?

EXT. TRAIN – LONG SHOT

As it speeds through the darkness.

CLOSE SHOT: THE DIESEL LOCOMOTIVE
As its horn blasts four times.

DISSOLVE TO:

INT. EVE'S DRAWING-ROOM – LATER

*The upper berth is closed now. Eve and Thornhill are standing close
together in the dark murmuring to each other between frequent kisses.
We hear them more than see them, for they are revealed to us only by
the passing lights outside the windows. Her back is against the wall near
the light switches. He is standing directly in front of her, his hands at her
waist. Her hands are at his shoulders, not helping, not resisting.*

EVE

You know, I've been thinking – it's not safe for you to roam
around Chicago looking for this George Kaplan you've been
telling me about. You'll be picked up by the police the
moment you show your face . . .

THORNHILL
(*kissing her*)
And it's such a nice face, too.

EVE
(*kissing him back*)
Don't you think it would be better if you stayed in my hotel
room while *I* located Mr Kaplan and brought him to you?

THORNHILL

Can't let you get involved. Too dangerous.

EVE

I'm a big girl.

THORNHILL
(*nibbling away*)

In all the right places, too.

EVE
(*responding with growing excitement*)

This is ridiculous. You *know* that, don't you?

THORNHILL
(*kissing her lips*)

Yes.

EVE

I mean, we've hardly *met*.

THORNHILL

That's right.

EVE

How do I know you *aren't* a murderer?

THORNHILL
(*to her neck*)

You don't.

EVE

Maybe you're planning to murder *me*, right here, tonight.

THORNHILL
(*working on her ear*)

Shall I?

EVE
(*whispers*)

Yes . . . please do . . .

This time her hands do help him, and it is a long kiss indeed.

THORNHILL

What's happening to us?

EVE

We're just strangers on a train.

THORNHILL

Beats flying, doesn't it?

EVE

We should stop.

THORNHILL
(*continuing*)

Immediately.

EVE

I ought to know more about you.

THORNHILL
(*kissing her*)

The rest is unimportant.

EVE

You're an advertising man, that's all I know. You've got taste in clothes . . . taste in food –

THORNHILL

Taste in women.
(*tasting her*)

I like your flavor

EVE

And you're very clever with words. You can probably make them do anything for you . . . Sell people things they don't need . . . Make women who don't know you fall in love with you . . .

THORNHILL

I'm beginning to think I'm underpaid.

And then they come together slowly in a long kiss that might never have ended if the door buzzer hadn't sounded. They break apart, look towards the door. Thornhill quickly steps inside the lavatory and closes the door, as Eve snaps on the overhead lights, goes to the other door, unlocks it and opens it. A Porter is standing there.

EVE
(*for Thornhill's ears*)
Oh – the porter. I suppose you want to make up my bed.

PORTER
(*entering*)
Yes, ma'am.

EVE
(*holding up the key*)
Is this yours? I found it on the floor.

PORTER
Why yes, ma'am. I've been looking all over for it.

As the Porter opens a lower berth and starts making up the bed, Eve takes up her handbag and says, for Thornhill's benefit:

EVE
I'll wait outside.

She starts to open her handbag as she goes out to the corridor.

INT. LAVATORY

Thornhill is looking at his face in the mirror and feeling his chin. He looks around at Eve's toiletries, sees a tiny ladies' safety razor and a tiny shaving brush. He picks the razor up and looks from it to himself in the mirror with blank expression. He gives a casual half turn as he hears the voices of Eve and the Porter.

EVE'S VOICE
Thank you, porter.

PORTER'S VOICE
Thank *you*, ma'am. Good night now.

EVE'S VOICE
Good night.

Then he hears the compartment door being closed and locked, and a knock on the lavatory door.

Come out, come out, wherever you are.

Thornhill opens the door and steps out.

INT. DRAWING-ROOM

                    EVE
            (*by way of explanation*)
The porter . . .

                    THORNHILL
            (*noticing the open bed*)
Uh huh . . .
            (*he snaps off the overhead lights*)
Now where were we?

                    EVE
            (*moving close*)
Here?

                    THORNHILL
            (*holding her*)
Ah.

They kiss.

                              (*murmurs*)
I see he opened the bed.

                                        EVE
Yes . . .

                                   THORNHILL
Only one bed.

                                        EVE
Yes . . .

                                   THORNHILL
I think it's a good omen. Don't you?

                                        EVE
                                      (*sighs*)
Wonderful.

                                   THORNHILL
Know what it means?

                                        EVE
                                    (*dreamily*)
Mmm.

                                   THORNHILL
                                     (*softly*)
Tell me.

                                        EVE
It means . . . that *you* . . .
                                (*she looks up at him*)
. . . are going to sleep on the floor . . .

He gives her a look.

                                   THORNHILL
Here. Take your omen back.

*Eve kisses him gently on the lips, and as she presses her cheek against
his, her expression sobers for a moment and her eyes turn to the door
thoughtfully.*

INT. TRAIN — ANOTHER CAR

Shooting down the corridor, we see the Porter moving away from us. In his right hand is a folded piece of white paper.

CLOSER ANGLE: SIDE VIEW OF PORTER
The camera is now travelling with him. When he comes to a stop before the door of a drawing-room, the camera continues to travel a bit while he presses the buzzer. Camera is now facing the Porter. The door opens. We do not see the occupant.

> PORTER
> (*holding out the piece of paper*)
> A message from the lady in car thirty-nine-oh-one.

A man's hand emerges and takes the note. The Porter turns and moves away.

INT. DRAWING-ROOM

The man's hands unfold the note and it fills the screen. It says:

> What do I do with him in the morning?
> [signed]
> Eve.

FULL SHOT. DRAWING-ROOM
Leonard, the secretary of Glen Cove, is closing the door, turning and handing the note to his master, Phillip Vandamm, the man whom Thornhill had mistakenly assumed at Glen Cove to be Lester Townsend. Over this, the sound of the diesel horn blasting four times.

FADE OUT:

FADE IN:

INT. TRAIN PLATFORM — LA SALLE STREET STATION, CHICAGO — MORNING

The Twentieth Century Limited has come to the end of its run. Moving camera reveals passengers getting off, luggage being unloaded by Pullman porters, Redcaps swarming over the platform, some of them boarding the train, others getting off with luggage in hand. And now

camera picks up the two Detectives who boarded the train the night before. They are conferring with other plain-clothesmen and uniformed police who have come to meet the train. The men disperse, eyeing the off-going passengers as they take up positions.

ANOTHER ANGLE
Eve is seen getting off the train. Behind her comes a Redcap carrying her luggage. As we dolly with them along the long, crowded platform towards the terminal, we see that, beneath the red hat and the uniform, the baggage-smasher is really Thornhill.

CLOSE SHOT: THE TWO DETECTIVES
As they see Eve.

POINT OF VIEW: FROM DETECTIVES
Eve approaching, followed by her 'Redcap'.

MOVING SHOT: THORNHILL AND EVE
Eve sees the Detectives up ahead. She slows down, lets Thornhill draw abreast of her as they walk.

EVE
(*sotto voce*)

Keep walking. I'll catch up.

THORNHILL

Yes, ma'am.

The two Detectives step into her path. She stops. Thornhill continues on.

FIRST DETECTIVE

Anything to report, Miss Kendall?

EVE
(*with enthusiasm*)

Why yes. I had a *fine* night's sleep.

FIRST DETECTIVE
(*shaking his head with annoyance*)

I mean did you happen to see the man we're looking for?

                              EVE
Mr Thornycroft?

                        FIRST DETECTIVE
Thornhill.

                              EVE
Oh . . . No . . . I'm awfully sorry.
                          (*she smiles*)
But good luck to you both.

She walks away. The two Detectives look after her with sour expression.

MOVING SHOT: EVE AND THORNHILL
*Eve catches up with her 'Redcap', moves abreast of him as he struggles
with the heavy luggage.*

                              EVE
How're we doing?

                          THORNHILL
                          (*exhausted*)
I may collapse any minute.

                              EVE
Not yet. First we have to run the gauntlet. Look.

MOVING POINT OF VIEW: FROM EVE AND THORNHILL
*Police are lined up along the platform up ahead, eyeing everyone who
passes.*

MOVING SHOT: EVE AND THORNHILL
*They move right along under the very eyes of the police, talking to each
other with a technique that would arouse the approval of any
ventriloquist:*

                          THORNHILL
                          (*sweating*)
I'm accustomed to having a load on . . . What *have* you got in
these bags?

                              EVE
Bowling balls – naturally.

THORNHILL

Which one of these has my suit in it?

EVE

The small zippered affair underneath your right arm.

THORNHILL

That ought to do it a lot of good.

EVE

I'm sure Mr Kaplan won't mind a few wrinkles.

THORNHILL

If he's still there. What time is it?

EVE

Nine-thirty.

THORNHILL

He may have left his hotel room by now.

EVE

I'll call him for you as soon as we get inside the station.

THORNHILL

No. I'll do it.

EVE

Redcap in a phone booth? Slightly suspicious.

THORNHILL

All right. You know what to tell him?

EVE

You want to see him right away. Terribly urgent. Matter of
life and death. No explanations.

THORNHILL

Good.

EVE

And while I'm calling, you change your clothes.

THORNHILL

Where do you propose I do that – in Marshall Field's
window?

EVE

I sort of had the Men's Room in mind.

THORNHILL
(*gives her a look*)
Did you now.
(*pause*)
You're the smartest girl I ever spent the night with on a train.

She glances at him with a slight smile. He gives her a sour look.

CLOSE-UP: EVE
As she looks straight ahead again, her expression becomes thoughtful with a trace of distress. She turns her head slightly.

EXT. PLATFORM

In a medium shot, we now see the subject of Eve's troubled thoughts: Vandamm and Leonard, who are getting off their Pullman car. They start to walk towards the camera.

CLOSE-UP: EVE
She glances at Thornhill with a trace of sadness in her eyes.

CLOSE-UP: THORNHILL (FROM EVE'S POINT OF VIEW)
With a cheerful eye cocked for any signs of danger ahead.

THE PLATFORM UP AHEAD (FROM THORNHILL'S POINT OF VIEW) – MOVING SHOT
There are no police in sight.

TWO SHOT: THORNHILL AND EVE

THORNHILL
Looks like we've made it.

SEMI-LONG SHOT: THE PLATFORM
There is a commotion around the steps of the car from which Eve and Thornhill alighted. On the top of the steps appears a hatless, middle-aged man in his underwear, socks and shoes. Behind him are two uniformed Policemen pushing him down the steps to the platform. Our

95

two Detectives quickly step forward to question him. At the same time, the two uniformed Police alight to the platform and complete the small knot of men surrounding the uniformless Redcap. For a moment we see the hapless Redcap gesticulating as he describes how he came to be in this state of undress. Then suddenly the Police and Detectives dash away and down the platform towards the main lobby, leaving the man standing there in his underwear.

CLOSE SHOT: THE REDCAP
He watches the departing police, then fishes out a few dollar bills from inside his underwear and counts them over.

INT. MAIN LOBBY – HIGH ANGLE SHOT

Much activity, many people, a profusion of Redcaps. If one of them is Thornhill, it is difficult to tell. Now we see the four minions of the law arriving in the lobby. They dash about, rounding up Redcaps, who submit to examination with much bewilderment. One Detective whips off a Redcap's hat. Angrily the man snatches it back. Another Detective spots a Redcap who is hurrying away, his back to camera. He looks very much like Thornhill from the rear. The Detective grabs him, whirls him around, and finds himself staring into a stunned, open mouthful of teeth that definitely do not answer to the description of Thornhill's.

INT. MEN'S ROOM

There is considerable activity here. At the row of wash basins stand three men. One is washing his hands, the other is scraping away at his chin with a straight razor, and the third man – Thornhill – is busily rubbing in a foamy lather which covers the lower half of his face. He is in his regular trousers by now, and his jacket hangs nearby. At his feet stands Eve's small zippered bag. The Redcap uniform is nowhere to be seen. Suddenly the door bursts open and our two Detectives enter. Thornhill and the other men turn at the commotion, casually watch the Detectives glancing about in search of their quarry. As Thornhill turns back to the mirror and continues to lather his face, we hear the sound of stall doors opening and banging closed. Their mission unaccomplished, the Detectives go out. Thornhill nonchalantly finishes his lathering, then looks down and picks up his razor, which, up to now, we have not seen. It is the tiny one belonging to Eve. He starts to draw it down his cheek, leaving the narrowest of lines down the lather. Then in the mirror he catches sight of the man with the straight razor staring at him in bewilderment.

EXT. PHONE BOOTH IN MAIN LOBBY

We see Eve through the glass doors, listening to someone on the phone, writing on a memo pad and saying a few words of agreement. The camera now begins to travel along the row of booths. We see various people at telephones. The camera comes to a stop outside another booth. Through the glass we see Leonard speaking. He seems to be issuing specific instructions, glances at his wrist-watch once. After a pause, he hangs up.

EXT. ROW OF BOOTHS

A raking shot of the line of booths, showing Eve in the foreground booth through the glass in the act of hanging up. She folds the piece of paper as she rises and emerges from the booth, her head turned away from us. Simultaneously, the door of Leonard's booth opens and he steps out. Without looking at Eve, he crosses over to Vandamm, who is idly glancing at a magazine at the news-stand. Leonard murmurs something to him, and the two men move off. Now Eve turns, looks about, and reacts as she sees:

LONG SHOT: POINT OF VIEW
Thornhill, carrying Eve's small zippered bag, is walking with assumed nonchalance across the station. He gives a deliberate side glance in Eve's direction, meaning: 'Follow me.'

SEMI-LONG SHOT:
Eve starts to move across the lobby after Thornhill.

CLOSE SHOT: THORNHILL
He is just coming to a stop at a secluded spot behind a column. He turns and waits. After a few moments, Eve comes into the shot. She has assumed a much lighter air. He hands her the zippered bag and several baggage tickets.

                            EVE
What took you so long?

                        THORNHILL
Small razor. Big face.
                    (*glancing about warily*)
Did you get Kaplan?

                            EVE
Yes.

                        THORNHILL
Good. What did he say?

                            EVE
He'll see you, but not at the hotel under any circumstances.
He'll meet you on the outside.

                        THORNHILL
Where? When?

                            EVE
I've got it all written out for you.

She hands him the slip of paper. He studies it as she talks.

You're to take the Greyhound Bus that leaves Chicago for
Indianapolis at two and ask the driver to let you off at the
Prairie Stop on Highway 41.

                        THORNHILL
                        (*reading*)
Prairie Stop . . . Highway 41 . . .

                            EVE
About an hour-and-a-half's drive from Chicago.

                        THORNHILL
I can rent a car.

                            EVE
No car. Mr Kaplan said bus. He wants to be sure you're
alone.

THORNHILL

All right. What do I do when I get there?

EVE

Just stand beside the road and wait. He'll be there at three-thirty.

THORNHILL

How will I know him?

EVE

He'll know *you*. You made the Chicago papers too.

THORNHILL

Ah.

EVE

Have you got your watch set to Central time?

THORNHILL

Yes.
                    (*looking at her*)
What's the matter?

EVE

Matter?

THORNHILL

You. You seem . . . I don't know . . . tense.

EVE
                    (*turns away*)
You better go. Before the police run out of Redcaps.

THORNHILL

We'll see each other again, won't we?

EVE
                    (*strained*)
Sometime . . . I'm sure . . .

THORNHILL
                    (*with tenderness*)
I never found a moment to thank you properly.

                              EVE
                          (*disturbed*)
Please go.

                          THORNHILL
But where will I find you?

                              EVE
                          (*evasively*)
I have to pick up my bags now . . .

He takes hold of her, turns her to him.

                          THORNHILL
Please wait a minute . . .

She looks past him.

                              EVE
They're coming.

*Thornhill, unable to see over his shoulder because of the column behind
him, gives half a glance and dashes off out of the shot. The camera eases
over and shoots past Eve's shoulder into the main lobby. There are no
police, just a few desultory travellers. Eve turns into the camera and
looks after the departed Thornhill with an unhappy expression.*

DISSOLVE TO:

EXT. HIGHWAY 41 – HELICOPTER SHOT – AFTERNOON

*We start close on a Greyhound bus, shooting down on it and travelling
along with it as it speeds in an easterly direction at 70 mph. Gradually,
camera draws away from the bus, going higher but never losing sight of
the vehicle, which recedes into the distance below and becomes a toy-like
object on an endless ribbon of deserted highway that stretches across
miles of flat prairie. Now the bus is slowing down. It is nearing a
junction where a small dirt road coming from nowhere crosses the
highway and continues on to nowhere. The bus stops. A man gets out. It
is Thornhill. But to us he is only a tiny figure. The bus starts away,
moves on out of sight. And now Thornhill stands alone beside the road –
a tiny figure in the middle of nowhere.*

EXT. ON THE GROUND

Thornhill glances about, studying his surroundings. The terrain is flat and treeless, even more desolate from this point than it seemed from the air. Here and there patches of low-growing farm crops add some contour to the land. A hot sun beats down. Utter silence hangs heavily in the air. Thornhill glances at his wrist-watch. It is 3:25.

In the distance, the faint hum of a motor vehicle is heard. Thornhill looks off to the west. The hum grows louder as the car draws nearer. Thornhill steps closer to the edge of the highway. A black sedan looms up, travelling at high speed. For a moment we are not sure it is not hurtling right at Thornhill. And then it zooms past him, recedes into the distance, becoming a faint hum, a tiny speck, and then silence again.

Thornhill takes out a handkerchief, mops his face. He is beginning to sweat now. It could be from nervousness, as well as the heat. Another faint hum, coming from the east, growing louder as he glances off and sees another distant speck becoming a speeding car, this one a closed convertible. Again, anticipation on Thornhill's face. Again, the vague uneasiness of indefinable danger approaching at high speed. And again, zoom – a cloud of dust – a car receding into the distance – a faint hum – and silence.

His lips tighten. He glances at his watch again. He steps out into the middle of the highway, looks first in one direction, then the other. Nothing in sight. He loosens his tie, opens his shirt collar, looks up at the sun. Behind him, in the distance, another vehicle is heard approaching. He turns, looks off to the west. This one is a huge transcontinental moving van, roaring towards him at high speed. With quick apprehension he moves off the highway to the dusty side of the road as the van thunders past and disappears. Its fading sound is replaced with a new sound, the chugging of an old flivver.

Thornhill looks off in the direction of the approaching sound, sees a flivver nearing the highway from the intersecting dirt road. When the car reaches the highway, it comes to a stop. A middle-aged woman is behind the wheel. Her passenger is a nondescript man of about fifty. He could certainly be a farmer. He gets out of the car. It makes a U-turn and drives off in the direction from which it came. Thornhill watches the man take up a position across the highway from him. The man glances

*at Thornhill without visible interest, then looks off up the highway
towards the east as if waiting for something to come along.*

Thornhill stares at the man, wondering if this is George Kaplan.

*The man looks idly across the highway at Thornhill, his face
expressionless.*

*Thornhill wipes his face with his handkerchief, never taking his eyes off
the man across the highway. The faint sound of an approaching plane
has gradually come up over the scene. As the sound grows louder,
Thornhill looks up to his left and sees a low-flying biplane approaching
from the northwest. He watches it with mounting interest as it heads
straight for the spot where he and the stranger face each other across the
highway. Suddenly it is upon them, only a hundred feet above the
ground, and then, like a giant bird, as Thornhill turns with the plane's
passage, it flies over them and continues on.*

*Thornhill stares after the plane, his back to the highway. When the
plane has gone several hundred yards beyond the highway, it loses
altitude, levels off only a few feet above the ground and begins to fly
back and forth in straight lines parallel to the highway, letting loose a
trail of powdered dust from beneath its fuselage as it goes. Any farmer
would recognize the operation as simple crop-dusting.*

*Thornhill looks across the highway, sees that the stranger is watching
the plane with idle interest. Thornhill's lips set with determination. He
crosses over and goes up to the Man.*

THORNHILL

Hot day.

MAN

Seen worse.

THORNHILL

Are you . . . uh . . . by any chance supposed to be meeting
someone here?

MAN
(still watching the plane)

Waitin' for the bus. Due any minute.

102

THORNHILL

Oh . . .

MAN
(*idly*)
Some of them crop-duster pilots get rich, if they live long
enough . . .

THORNHILL
Then your name isn't . . . Kaplan.

MAN
(*glances at him*)
Can't say it is, 'cause it ain't.
(*he looks off up the highway*)
Well – here she comes, right on time.

*Thornhill looks off to the east, sees a Greyhound bus approaching. The
Man peers off at the plane again, and frowns.*

That's funny.

THORNHILL
What?

MAN
That plane's dustin' crops where there ain't no crops.

*Thornhill looks across at the droning plane with growing suspicion as
the stranger steps out onto the highway and flags the bus to a stop.
Thornhill turns towards the stranger as though to say something to him.
But it is too late. The man has boarded the bus, its doors are closing and
it is pulling away. Thornhill is alone again.*

*Almost immediately, he hears the plane engine being gunned to a higher
speed. He glances off sharply, sees the plane veering off its parallel course
and heading towards him. He stands there wide-eyed, rooted to the spot.
The plane roars on, a few feet off the ground. There are two men in the
twin cockpits, goggled, unrecognizable, menacing. He yells out to them,
but his voice is lost in the noise of the plane. In a moment it will be upon
him and decapitate him. Desperately he drops to the ground and presses
himself flat as the plane zooms over him with a great noise, almost
combing his hair with a landing wheel.*

Thornhill scrambles to his feet, sees the plane banking and turning. He looks about wildly, sees a telephone pole and dashes for it as the plane comes at him again. He ducks behind the pole. The plane heads straight for him, veers to the right at the last moment. We hear two sharp cracks of gunfire mixed with the sound of the engine, as two bullets slam into the pole just above Thornhill's head.

Thornhill reacts to this new peril, sees the plane banking for another run at him. A car is speeding along the highway from the west. Thornhill dashes out onto the road, tries to flag the car down but the driver ignores him and races by, leaving him exposed and vulnerable as the plane roars in on him. He dives into a ditch and rolls away as another series of shots are heard and bullets rake the ground that he has just occupied.

He gets to his feet, looks about, sees a cornfield about fifty yards from the highway, glances up at the plane making its turn, and decides to make a dash for the cover of the tall-growing corn.

Shooting down from a helicopter about one hundred feet above the ground, we see Thornhill running towards the cornfield and the plane in pursuit.

Shooting from within the cornfield, we see Thornhill come crashing in, scuttling to the right and lying flat and motionless as we hear the plane zoom over him with a burst of gunfire and bullets rip into the corn, but at a safe distance from Thornhill. He raises his head cautiously, gasping for breath, as he hears the plane move off and into its turn.

Shooting down from the helicopter, we see the plane levelling off and starting a run over the cornfield, which betrays no sign of the hidden Thornhill. Skimming over the top of the cornstalks, the plane gives forth no burst of gunfire now. Instead, it lets loose thick clouds of poisonous dust which settle down into the corn.

Within the cornfield, Thornhill, still lying flat, begins to gasp and choke as the poisonous dust envelops him. Tears stream from his eyes but he does not dare move as he hears the plane coming over the field again. When the plane zooms by and another cloud of dust hits him, he jumps to his feet and crashes out into the open, half blinded and gasping for breath. Far off down the highway to the right, he sees a huge diesel gasoline-tanker approaching. He starts running towards the highway to intercept it.

Shooting from the helicopter, we see Thornhill dashing for the highway, the plane levelling off for another run at him, and the diesel tanker speeding closer.

Shooting across the highway, we see Thornhill running and stumbling towards camera, the plane closing in behind him, and the diesel tanker approaching from the left. He dashes out into the middle of the highway and waves his arms wildly.

The diesel tanker thunders down the highway towards Thornhill, klaxon blasting impatiently.

The plane speeds relentlessly towards Thornhill from the field bordering the highway.

Thornhill stands alone and helpless in the middle of the highway, waving his arms. The plane draws closer. The tanker is almost upon him. It isn't going to stop. He can hear the klaxon blasting him out of the way. There is nothing he can do. The plane has caught up with him. The tanker won't stop. It's got to stop. He hurls himself to the pavement directly in its path. There is a scream of brakes and skidding tires, the roar of the plane engine and then a tremendous boom as the diesel truck grinds to a stop inches from Thornhill's body just as the plane, hopelessly committed and caught unprepared by the sudden stop, slams into the travelling gasoline tanker and plane and gasoline explode into a great sheet of flame.

In the next few moments, all is confusion. Thornhill, unhurt, rolls out from under the wheels of the diesel truck. The drivers clamber out of the front seat and drop to the highway. Black clouds of smoke billow up from the funeral pyre of the plane and its cremated occupants. We recognize the flaming body of one of the men in the plane. It is Licht, one of Thornhill's original abductors.

An elderly open pick-up truck with a second-hand refrigerator standing in it, which has been approaching from the east, pulls up at the side of the road. Its driver, a farmer, jumps out and hurries towards the wreckage.

FARMER

What happened? What happened?

The diesel truck drivers are too dazed to answer. Flames and smoke drive them all back. Thornhill, unnoticed, heads towards the unoccupied pick-up truck. Another car comes up from the west, stops, and its driver runs towards the other men. They stare, transfixed, at the holocaust. Suddenly, from behind them, they hear the pick-up truck's motor starting. The farmer who owns the truck turns, and is startled to see his truck being driven away by an utter stranger.

    Hey!

He runs after the truck. But the stranger – who is Thornhill – steps harder on the accelerator and speeds off in the direction of Chicago.

    DISSOLVE TO:

EXT. MICHIGAN AVENUE, CHICAGO – NIGHT

The abandoned pick-up truck, with its lonely refrigerator, stands incongruously parked among some new and elegant cars. A patrolman has opened the door and is peering inside.

EXT. STREET NEAR HOTEL AMBASSADOR EAST

A police squad car is cruising slowly past the entrances to the Ambassador East and Ambassador West, which face each other on opposite sides of the street. Inside the car, two police lieutenants glance about, eyes searching the area. Camera whips to Thornhill, standing in an attitude of concealment inside the doorway of a darkened store as he watches the police car drive on. He looks quite dishevelled, and his suit would not pass muster at, say, Twenty-One. Now he steps to the sidewalk and starts walking in the direction of the Ambassador East.

EXT. ENTRANCE HOTEL AMBASSADOR EAST

Thornhill approaches the hotel and enters.

INT. LOBBY HOTEL AMBASSADOR EAST

Thornhill crosses the lobby to the desk and waits for a Clerk to come over.

                    CLERK
               (eyeing him with distaste)
    Yes?

THORNHILL

Could you let me have Mr George Kaplan's room number, please?

CLERK
(*thoughtfully*)

Kaplan . . .

(*as he starts to one side to consult files*)
I think he checked out . . .

THORNHILL

Checked out?

CLERK
(*returns with a file card*)
That's right. Checked out at seven-ten this morning.

THORNHILL

Seven-ten? Are you sure?

CLERK

Yes. Left a forwarding address – Hotel Sheraton-Johnson, Rapid City, South Dakota.

Thornhill has taken out the slip of paper on which Eve had given him directions to meet Kaplan.

THORNHILL
(*talking half to himself*)
Seven-ten? Then how come I got a message from him at nine-thir–?

CLERK

What was that?

THORNHILL

Nothing, nothing.

His eyes narrow and his jaw tightens with realization. He crumples the piece of paper into a ball and hurls it away in anger. Just then he looks up and sees Eve, who has come through the entrance to the lobby. She does not see him as she goes directly to the news-stand and buys an evening paper. Thornhill draws back, watches her unobserved as she glances quickly at the front page while hurrying to a waiting elevator. She steps

108

in, the door closes and the elevator starts up. Thornhill watches the floor indicator until the elevator stops. Then he turns back to the Clerk.

THORNHILL

Sorry to bother you again.

CLERK

Uh-huh.

THORNHILL

Miss Eve Kendall is expecting me. Room four-something-or-other. I've forgotten the number. Would you mind?

The Clerk steps to one side, examines his listings, then returns to Thornhill.

CLERK

She's in four sixty-three.

THORNHILL

Thanks.

He hurries towards the elevator as the Clerk looks after him.

QUICK DISSOLVE TO:

HOTEL CORRIDOR. FOURTH FLOOR

Thornhill approaches the door to 463, looks up and down the corridor if for no other reason than to indicate to us that he has now become suspicious, cautious and surreptitious in matters pertaining to Eve. He puts an ear to her door, listens, hears nothing. He presses the buzzer and waits. Presently the door opens and she sees him standing before her. Her eyes widen. She is too stunned to say anything.

THORNHILL
(*pleasantly*)

Hello.

He goes right past her into the room.

INT. EVE'S HOTEL ROOM

Eve turns, stares at Thornhill as she closes the door behind him. If his back were not to her, he would see the mixed emotions on her face – not just surprise, but overwhelming relief, too. But relief is not something she can afford to reveal too strongly, because that would indicate that there was something to be relieved about. *She is almost completely controlled by the time Thornhill turns to her, after a very brief moment in which his darting glance has taken in the room, and the open door to the bathroom, and noticed nothing worthy of apprehension.*

THORNHILL

Surprised?

EVE

Yes.

She stares at him, still shaken.

THORNHILL

No getting rid of *me*, is there?

Suddenly Eve goes up to him, puts her arms around him, holds him close and presses her face to his breast. Is it tenderness and relief, or merely the need to hide from the double-edged meaning of his last remark? Thornhill puts his hands on her, but without affection. He knows he is on to something now, and he intends to play it cool. Occasionally his deep down anger will make him say incautious things he oughtn't to say if he intends to disarm the girl – and just as occasionally, he will be even warmer than he intended to be. He can't help liking this female a little bit, even while he would like to slug her. It's because he remembers last night. It's because, also, she happens to be of the opposite sex.

I need a drink.

EVE

I have some scotch.

THORNHILL

With water. No ice.

Eve disengages herself from him and goes over to a table where drinking things are set up. Thornhill takes the opportunity to saunter over to a chair where the newspaper has been thrown. The front-page story is plainly visible:

TWO DIE AS CROP-DUSTER PLANE CRASHES
Low-flying craft hits oil tanker.
Truck drivers escape holocaust.

During this, and while Eve is mixing drinks, they are talking:

                        EVE
                  (*too casually*)
How did it go today?

                     THORNHILL
The meeting with Kaplan?

                        EVE
Uh-huh.

                     THORNHILL
                  (*just as casually*)
He didn't show up.

                        EVE
Oh?

                     THORNHILL
                 (*staring at her back*)
Funny, isn't it?

                        EVE
                (*after a slight pause*)
Why funny?

                     THORNHILL
After all those very involved and very explicit directions he
gave you on the phone.

                        EVE
Maybe I copied them down wrong.

                     THORNHILL
I don't think you got them wrong. I think you sent me to the
right place all right.

*He couldn't resist that one. Fortunately for Eve, her face is not turned to
him, and she can always fumble with glasses and stirring rods.*

EVE

Why not call him again and see what happened?

THORNHILL

I did. He checked out, went to South Dakota.

EVE

South Dakota?

THORNHILL

Rapid City.

EVE
(*after a moment*)

What are you going to do next?

THORNHILL

I haven't made up my mind yet. It may depend on you.

On this, Eve turns, with the drinks in her hands.

EVE

On me?

She walks up to him.

THORNHILL

You're my little helper, aren't you?

He takes a glass from her, all the while staring into her eyes.

To us.
(*he touches his glass to hers*)
To a long and lasting friendship . . .
(*he takes a sip*)
Meaning, from now on, I'm not going to let *you* out of my sight, sweetheart.

EVE
(*hiding in her glass*)

I'm afraid you're going to have to, Thornhill.

THORNHILL
(*shakes his head*)

Unh-uh.

EVE
(*turning away*)
I do have plans of my own, you know – and you do have
problems.

*Thornhill takes a long drag on his drink before he speaks, and once
again he engraves each word on a Gillette Blue Blade.*

THORNHILL
Wouldn't it be nice if my problems and your plans were
somehow . . . *connected?*
(*her quick glance finds his face smiling softly, nay lovingly*)
Then we could stay close to each other from here on in and
not have to go off in separate directions. Togetherness. Know
what I mean?

*Eve stares at him for a moment saying nothing, and is saved by the bell
as the phone rings. She glances at it, but makes no move to answer it.*

Go ahead. It can't be for *me.*

*She hesitates uncertainly. The phone rings again. He makes a move as
though he will answer it. Quickly Eve walks over to the night-table
between the beds and picks up the phone, while Thornhill saunters
around the room just as though he were not utterly alert and keenly
interested in every monosyllable of her tightly-controlled conversation.*

EVE
(*to phone*)
Hello?
(*listens*)
Yes.
(*listens*)
No, don't. I'm not dressed yet.
(*listens*)
What time?
(*listens*)
I'll meet you.
(*listens*)
What's the address?

She takes up a pencil, writes something down on a memo pad as she listens. Thornhill observes this out of the corner of his glance.

All right.

> *(listens)*

I will.

> *(listens)*

Goodbye.

She hangs up, tears off the page on which she has written something, walks over to her handbag on the dresser and puts the slip of paper inside. We see a gun in her handbag.

THORNHILL
Business?

EVE
Yes.

THORNHILL
Industrial designing business?

EVE
Mm hmmm.

He goes up behind her, puts his hands about her waist. (The nice thing about this kind of cat-and-mouse work is that you can enjoy yourself while you're doing it, because it's part of the game.) Eve is disturbed by the nearness of him, and his hands on her.

THORNHILL
All work and no play. Girl like you should be enjoying herself tonight instead of taking phone calls from clients. How about dinner with *me* just for openers?

EVE
You can't afford to be seen anywhere.

THORNHILL
What's wrong with up here? Our own little Pump Room for two.

Eve pulls out of his grasp, moves away from him.

EVE
No . . . I . . . I can't.

THORNHILL
(*easily*)

I insist.

Eve is in a spot. She gets control of herself before she turns to him. But a little desperation does creep through in her voice.

EVE

I want you to do me a favor, Thornhill – a big, big favor.

THORNHILL

Name it.

EVE

I want you to leave, right now. Stay far away from me and don't come near me again. We're *not* going to get involved. Last night was last night and that's all there was, that's all there is, there isn't going to be anything more between us. So please – goodbye, good luck, no conversation. Just leave.

THORNHILL
(*utterly unperturbed*)

Right away?

EVE

Yes.

THORNHILL

No questions asked?

EVE

Yes.

Thornhill looks at her a moment. She wants to get rid of him. She's got to get rid of him. That's for sure. He shakes his head.

THORNHILL

Unh-uh.

EVE

Please . . .

THORNHILL

After dinner.

EVE

Now.

THORNHILL

(*firmly*)

After dinner. Fair is fair.

Eve's lips tighten, but she is careful not to betray the urgency of her situation. The wheels go round for a moment as she looks at him. Then, she makes a decision, softens her expression, and smiles.

EVE

All right. On one condition.

(*she goes up to him, touches his rumpled, dirty suit*)

You've got to let the hotel valet do something with that suit first. You belong in the *stockyards* looking like that.

THORNHILL

(*shrugs*)

I'm very large with pigs this year.

EVE

(*pointing*)

There's the phone.

She turns to the mirror and starts to fix her hair. Thornhill goes over to the bed, sits down and puts his hand on the phone but doesn't pick it up. He is thinking fast. With a cautious glance over his shoulder, he slides his hand to the memo pad beside the phone and tilts it slightly. He sees something there on the pad but we do not see what it is. Now he picks up the phone.

THORNHILL

(*to phone*)

Valet service, please . . . Valet? This is . . . uh . . .

(*to Eve*)

Where are we?

EVE

Four sixty-three.

THORNHILL
(*to phone*)
This is room four sixty-three. How long would it take to get a suit sponged and pressed real fast? . . . Twenty minutes? Fine . . . Four sixty-three.
(*he hangs up*)
He'll be right up.

EVE
Better take your things off.

THORNHILL
(*going up to her*)
What am I going to do with my clothes off for twenty minutes?
(*an afterthought, as he gazes at her reflection in the mirror*)
Couldn't he take an *hour*?

EVE
(*turns, practically in his arms*)
You could always take a cold shower.

She starts to help him off with his jacket as he takes his things out of his pockets and places them on the dresser. Both of them are playing it just as though they were up to nothing but good, clean, healthy love-play.

THORNHILL
When I was a little boy, I never even let my *mother* undress me.

EVE
(*peeling off the jacket*)
Well, you're a big boy now.

She tosses the jacket on the bed, turns back to him, puts her hands on his belt buckle, starts to unfasten it. He takes her hands in his.

THORNHILL
How did a girl like you ever get to be a girl like you?

EVE
Lucky, I guess.

117

THORNHILL

Not lucky – wicked . . . naughty . . . up to no good . . . Ever
kill anyone?

*Instantly Eve's expression changes. He has gone dangerously too far;
quickly he takes the curse off the remark.*

Bet you could tease a man to death without even trying.
>   (*he pats her cheek*)

So stop trying, hm?

*He starts towards the bathroom, undoing the belt buckle himself as he
goes. The door buzzer sounds. Eve goes to the door, opens it, lets the
valet in.*

EVE
(*to the valet*)

Be right with you.
>   (*she goes to the half open bathroom door*)

Trousers, please.

*Thornhill's hand comes out with the trousers. Eve takes them, picks up
the jacket on the bed, gives the suit to the valet and closes the door
behind him. From the bathroom she hears Thornhill's voice calling out
to her:*

THORNHILL'S VOICE

Think I'll take that cold shower after all.

EVE

Good.

*Next she hears the shower being turned on, then Thornhill's voice raised
in a loud, shower-stall rendition of 'The Night They Invented
Champagne'. Immediately, and with urgent haste, Eve prepares to
leave. She goes to the closet, gets the jacket of her suit, puts it on. Then
from a dresser drawer she takes some papers and stuffs them into her
handbag, darting occasional glances towards the partially open
bathroom door from whence comes Thornhill's 'Singin' in the Rain'.*

*Her glance falls on Thornhill's belongings, which he had removed from
his pockets. A closer view of them shows the torn newspaper photograph
of Vandamm covered by Thornhill's 'ROT' initialled matchbook. Eve's*

hand sets the matches aside, picks up the torn newspaper photograph, holds it long enough for quick study and puts it down again. In a wider angle she turns, and, with a final glance around, starts out of the room.

INT. BATHROOM

Thornhill is not in the shower after all. In shirt, tie, shorts, socks and shoes, he has been standing at the crack in the door peering out at Eve's furtive activities while singing lustily, the shower spraying away busily behind him. Now he hears the outer door close as Eve makes her hasty exit.

CLOSE SHOT: THORNHILL

As he opens the bathroom door wider, steps out into the room. It is clear from his expression that he has not really been duped, but rather has been ahead of this little game all along. He goes to the night-table, picks up the memo pad on which Eve had made a notation and removed the top sheet. He picks up a pencil and in a closer angle we see him trace in the indentation left by Eve's pencil. It reads: '1212 N. MICHIGAN'.

DISSOLVE TO:

EXT. MICHIGAN AVE., CHICAGO – NIGHT

A taxi pulls up and Thornhill steps out. (His suit is in fine shape now.) He glances about, sees that he has the right address, and moves across the sidewalk.

CLOSER ANGLE – EXT. SHAW & OPPENHEIM GALLERIES

The lighted window of a rather elegant art gallery. A sign in the window announces:

'AUCTION TONIGHT – 8:00 P.M.
FURNITURE AND OBJETS D'ART FROM
THE COLLECTION OF DR ORLANDO MENDOZA'

Over the door, the building number: '1212'. *Thornhill frowns, puzzled, takes out the slip of paper, looks up at the number again, then decides to go inside.*

AUCTIONEER

Thank you, sir. Four hundred fifty dollars is bid for the pair, can I hear five hundred, will you say five hundred, can I say the five hundred, fair warning and last call – sold to Mr Stone second row.

On the stage the chairs are removed as lot 103, an Aubusson settee is brought onto the stage.

CLOSE SHOT: *Vandamm's fingers gently moving over the soft flesh of Eve's neck. Camera draws back to include Eve seated, Vandamm standing behind her and Leonard beyond them seated on a low table, his legs dangling. At the far end of the room is a raised platform on which an Auctioneer and his Assistant, with the aid of portable microphones, are going about the business of unloading various objets d'art. Elderly men in black dust-jackets pass the items from the wings on to the stage, one piece at a time, where each object is then auctioned off at the leisurely pace which distinguishes the sale of nineteenth-century French paintings from the sale of twentieth-century American tobacco. Most of the hundred-odd spectators at the auction are seated on folding chairs in the center of the room. Moving along the aisle on either side of them are several handsome young women employed by the gallery to jot down the names of successful bidders, should they not be known. Beyond these aisles, on either side, is the overflow of spectators, some of them seated, some standing, others leaning against antique period furniture.*

Lot number 103. Ah! this lovely Aubusson settee, in excellent condition, please start the bidding. How much? Eight hundred dollars is offered, thank you. Eight hundred is bid, say the nine, go nine hundred. Nine hundred is bid, now who'll say one thousand? One thousand, thank you, one thousand, at one thousand, say eleven hundred, bid the eleven hundred, not enough for this choice piece, can I hear eleven hundred? Selling at one thousand, once at one thousand, twice, last call. Do I hear eleven hundred? Sold! One thousand to Mrs Sheridan.

The settee is removed from the stage and lot 104, a barometer, is brought in.

Lot number 104 – This eighteenth-century hand-carved barometer. Can I say two hundred and fifty to start? That gentleman says one hundred and fifty. I have one hundred and fifty. Say two hundred, two hundred is bid here, now go the three

Camera reaches the end of the dolly and pans to Thornhill, standing in entrance, staring off at Vandamm and the others. Thornhill's mouth tightens with anger. It is not that he is overwhelmed with surprise at this visible evidence of alliance, but it does remove any lingering doubts he might still have had about the girl. He has really been taken for a ride – almost, but not quite, all the way. And now, those fingers playing at the back of her neck. The hell with caution, and concealing anger. Besides, it's too late. He moves out of shot.

Thornhill moves to a chair near the group.

THORNHILL
The three of you together. Now there's a picture only Charles Addams could draw.

VANDAMM
(*imperturbed*)
Good evening, Mr Kaplan –

THORNHILL
(*bitterly*)
Before we start calling each other names, maybe you better tell me yours. I haven't had the pleasure.

VANDAMM
– You disappoint me, sir . . .

hundred, say three hundred, three hundred is bid, thank you. Do I hear three hundred and fifty? Three hundred and fifty, may I have three hundred and fifty, three hundred, three hundred twice, third and last call. Do I hear three hundred and fifty? Sold! Mr Echart three hundred.

The barometer is removed and lot 105 is brought in.

THORNHILL
(*bitterly at Eve*)
I was just going to say that to *her*.

Eve stares straight ahead. Vandamm gazes off at the Auctioneer.

VANDAMM
I've always understood you to be a pretty shrewd fellow at your job. What possessed you to come blundering in here like this? Could it be an overpowering interest in art?

THORNHILL
Yes. The art of survival.
(*a quick shaft at Leonard*)
Poured any good drunks lately?

EVE
(*in a hollow voice, to Vandamm*)
He followed me here from
the hotel.

LEONARD
(*to Eve*)
He was in your room?

*She nods. Vandamm reacts with
displeasure.*

THORNHILL
(*with contempt*)
Sure. Isn't everybody?

Now, ladies and gentlemen – number 105, an excellent example of pre-Columbian art. It dates from about 1000 AD. A Tarascan warrior from the State of Kolemia, in Mexico. May I hear a starting bid worthy of this fine art piece? Who will say one thousand dollars to start? The gentleman here suggests five hundred. All right, that's a start. Now say one thousand. I have five hundred dollars, may I say the thousand? Seven hundred and fifty is offered. Thank you, now say the thousand. One thousand is bid, make it twelve hundred and fifty. Eleven hundred, you say? All right I have eleven hundred bid, make it twelve hundred – twelve hundred dollars there. Now

At this time, the Auctioneer's voice is heard announcing item number 105. He proceeds to describe it. During this, an attendant has been walking about showing the figure to the spectators. Leonard taps the momentarily distracted Vandamm on the shoulder and points to the figure. Vandamm glances at it quickly, looks up at Leonard and says:

VANDAMM
Yes.

THORNHILL
(*to Vandamm*)
I didn't realize you were an art collector. I thought you just collected corpses.

The bidding has started.

VANDAMM
(*to Leonard, quietly*)
Fifteen hundred.

thirteen is here, fourteen hundred is bid.
(off-screen)
Fifteen hundred I'm bid, who'll say seventeen fifty – do I hear seventeen fifty?

Seventeen fifty is bid. Say two thousand – two thousand anyone – do I hear two thousand? Seventeen fifty is bid. Seventeen fifty, are you all through at seventeen fifty? Sold then to Mr Vandamm at seventeen fifty.

The Tarascan piece is removed and lot 106, a Louis XV curio cabinet is brought in.

Number 106 – for your pleasure is this Louis XV curio cabinet of gold and bronze doré with Vernis Martin figured decorations and landscape painting. Who will say five hundred dollars

Leonard makes a silent signal to the auctioneer.

  THORNHILL
 (*looking down at Eve*)
I'll bet you paid plenty for this little piece of –
sculpture –

  VANDAMM
 (*to Leonard*)
Seventeen fifty.

Eve is visibly suffering.

  THORNHILL
 (*continuing*)
She's worth every dollar, take it from me. She really puts her heart into her work. In fact her whole body.
 (*a quick glance at Leonard*)
And where does he keep *you* – in a curio cabinet?

Thornhill reacts to the Auctioneer's mention of Vandamm's name.

 (*hearing the name*)
Vandamm, huh?

  VANDAMM
 (*turns to Thornhill*)
Has anyone ever told you that you overplay your various roles rather severely, Mr Kaplan? First you're the outraged Madison Avenue man who claims he has been mistaken for someone else.

to start the bidding? Five hundred dollars for it. Five hundred dollars for it. All right I'll accept your start of two hundred dollars, two hundred is bid, go three, two fifty I have, say three, two fifty I have, say three hundred, three hundred now go four, three go four, three go four, three go four, three go four, three twenty-five is bid, say fifty, three fifty I have, say four, three hundred and fifty, go four hundred, three hundred and fifty, say three seventy-five, three hundred fifty, say seventy-five. Don't lose it for twenty-five dollars; thank you three hundred and seventy-five is bid. I have three hundred and seventy-five dollars, go the four hundred. Three seventy-five, go four. Four hundred dollars is bid. Say four hundred and twenty-five. Four hundred twenty-five once, four hundred twenty-five twice, last call at four hundred twenty-five. Sold to the lady in the fourth row for four hundred dollars.

The Louis XV cabinet is removed and lot 107 is brought in.

And now, ladies and gentlemen, we offer Catalogue number 107 – this

Then you play a fugitive from justice, supposedly trying to clear his name of a crime he knows he didn't commit. And now, you play the peevish lover, stung by jealousy and betrayal.
(*a chilly smile*)
Seems to me you fellows could stand a little less training from the FBI and a little more from the Actors' Studio.

THORNHILL
Apparently the only performance that's going to satisfy *you* is when I play dead.

VANDAMM
(*gently*)
Your very next role. You will be quite convincing, I assure you.

Leonard has already started out of the room to arrange that.

THORNHILL
(*watching him go*)
I wonder what subtle form of manslaughter is next on the program. Am I going to be dropped into a vat of molten steel and become part of some new skyscraper?
(*looking at Eve*)
Or are you going to ask *this* . . . female to kiss me again and *poison* me to death?

rare Marcolini Meissen compote, acquired by Dr Mendoza from the estate of the Comtesse de Chivre. How much to start the bidding on this collector's porcelain? Five hundred, madam? That's an extremely low start and should prompt spirited bidding. Six? Six hundred I have, now the seven, seven hundred I have, thank you, say eight. May I direct your attention to the magnificent *répoussé* flowers on this outstanding example. Eight hundred dollars there, nine hundred in the front. One thousand is bid on the far side. Eleven hundred dollars is here now, say the twelve, twelve hundred dollars there. Twelve hundred is bid, say thirteen hundred, may I hear thirteen hundred please? Fair selling at twelve hundred. Do I hear thirteen hundred? Last call, sold twelve hundred dollars. Thank you.

The Marcolini Meissen compote is removed and lot 108, the Vienna plates, is displayed.

Number 108 – we offer you now twelve Royal Vienna

Eve gets to her feet, turns and slaps him in the face. He grabs her wrists and they stare at each other for a moment.

(*with contempt*)
Who are you kidding? You *have* no feelings to hurt.

He firmly presses her back down into her seat. During this, a man in the audience nearby is half turned, as though he has been observing the entire altercation. It is the Professor of the CIA.

VANDAMM
(*angrily*)
Mr Kaplan –

THORNHILL
(*turning on him*)
Look, Vandamm, I don't know why you want me dead, but this I –

VANDAMM
(*interrupting*)
– We've had just about enough of you . . .

THORNHILL
Then why don't you call the police? No – that's the last thing you want – me in the hands of the police. There's something I might tell them, huh? That's why you had this one here hustle me on the train last night, like the good little industrial designer that she is. Well, something tells

plates, magnificently hand-decorated with portraits of Court beauties. How much a piece and take the lot? Thirty a piece is bid all over the house. Thirty-five, say forty, forty go forty-five, forty-five I have, go fifty – fifty go five, fifty go five, fifty is here, say fifty-five, fifty dollars a piece, say fifty-five, anymore, sir? Sold then for fifty dollars a piece.

The plates are taken out as a painting is brought in.

Catalogue number 109. A superb example of this early nineteenth-century master. It will enhance any collection of fine art. What is your pleasure? How much to start? One thousand is bid, twelve-fifty I have, fifteen hundred, fifteen hundred is bid, say seventeen fifty, I have seventeen fifty, two thousand is bid –

me I've got a much better chance of survival if I *go* to the police. And the mere fact that you don't *want* me to is enough for me.

(*to Eve*)
Goodnight, sweetheart. Don't think it hasn't been nice.

He walks away from them and goes towards the entrance in the rear. But he doesn't get very far before he stops. Standing inside the doorway waiting for him is Valerian, the UN assassin. Thornhill turns, looks about, and sees down the aisle, the steps to the Auctioneer's stage where men are bringing on a piece of furniture for auction. He starts down the aisle with the intention of making his way out through the back. Then he slows down as he sees Leonard stepping out of the 'wings' of the stage. Leonard looks at him steadily, and then withdraws significantly. Thornhill looks about him with desperation, then quickly slips into a nearby seat among the spectators. At this moment, Vandamm and Eve depart. Thornhill turns his attention to the platform, where the Auctioneer has a painting on the block.

(NOTE: Pick up dialogue in script.)

> AUCTIONEER

I have two thousand. Do I hear twenty-five? . . . Twenty-five hundred please . . . Twenty-two fifty. Thank you. Do I hear twenty-five? . . . Twenty-two fifty once. Twenty-two fifty twice. Last call . . .

> THORNHILL
> (*shouts*)

Fifteen hundred!

> AUCTIONEER
> (*startled*)

The bid is already up to twenty-two fifty, sir.

> THORNHILL

I *still* say fifteen hundred!

Heads turn towards him angrily. But Thornhill is concerned only about escaping the fate Valerian and Leonard have reserved for him.

> AUCTIONEER
> (*recovering*)

I have twenty-two fifty. Do I hear twenty-five hundred? . . . Twenty-two fifty once. Twenty-two fifty twice . . .

> THORNHILL

Twelve hundred!

> AUCTIONEER
> (*quickly*)

Sold for twenty-two fifty. And now –

> THORNHILL
> (*loudly*)

Twenty-two fifty for *that chromo*?

> AUCTIONEER
> (*ignoring him*)

– Number 116 in the catalogue . . .
> (*as attendants bring out a chaise longue*)

'A Louis XIV carved and painted *lit de repos*.' Kindly observe the moulded frame, the carved, freestanding columns at each corner and the fluted, tapering legs. Will somebody start the bidding at seven hundred and fifty dollars, please?

THORNHILL

How do we know it's not a fake? It *looks* like a fake!

An elderly Woman seated directly in front of Thornhill turns and glares at him.

WOMAN

One thing we know: *you're* no fake. You're a *genuine* idiot.

THORNHILL

Thank you.

AUCTIONEER

I wonder if I could respectfully ask the gentleman to get into the spirit of the proceedings here.

THORNHILL

All right. I'll start it at eight.

AUCTIONEER

Eight hundred dollars. Thank you. Nine hundred . . . One thousand I have. Go twelve.

THORNHILL

Eleven!

AUCTIONEER

Eleven is bid. Go twelve. Who'll say twelve? Eleven once Who'll say twelve? Eleven twice. Twelve. Thank you. Twelve is bid. I have twelve. Go thirteen. Who'll say thirteen?

THORNHILL

Thirteen dollars!

AUCTIONEER

You mean thirteen hundred, sir?

THORNHILL

I mean thirteen *dollars*, which is more than it's worth!

The Auctioneer will continue his work, but his assistant will now reach for the phone on his desk and make a hurried call, which will not go unnoticed by Thornhill.

AUCTIONEER

Twelve hundred I have. Go thirteen. Who'll say thirteen?
Twelve fifty? Twelve hundred once. Twelve hundred twice.
Last call. Twelve hundred.

THORNHILL

Two thousand!

AUCTIONEER
(*a little stunned*)

Two thousand?

THORNHILL

Twenty-one hundred!

AUCTIONEER

I'm sorry, sir, but we can't –

THORNHILL

Make it twenty-five hundred!

*By this time an angry murmur is rising from the spectators. Someone
shouts: 'Ask him to leave!' A uniformed male Attendant is moving
down the aisle towards Thornhill. Valerian and Leonard, in their
separate positions, are glancing about uncertainly.*

AUCTIONEER

Would the gentleman *please* cooperate?

ASSISTANT AUCTIONEER
(*trying to restore order*)

The last bid was twelve hundred.

THORNHILL

Twenty-five hundred! My money is as good as anybody's!

AUCTIONEER

I have twelve hundred once . . . twelve hundred twice . . .

THORNHILL

Three thousand!

AUCTIONEER

Last call. Sold for twelve hundred.

THORNHILL
(*leaping to his feet*)
You're not going to get away with this!

By this time the uniformed Attendant has reached Thornhill's row of seats, pushed into the row and grabbed him by the arm.

Let go of me! Get your hands off me or I'll sue!

Now the place is really in an uproar. Spectators push Thornhill into the aisle. He grapples with the Attendant as women cry out in alarm. Two Police Officers come running in through the entrance. Thornhill notices this with a pleased expression, hauls back and lets the Attendant have a good one on the jaw. The man goes reeling back into the crowd, bounces back and lets fly a swing at Thornhill, who ducks, moves in and wrestles him to the floor. During this, just after the police arrive, the Professor gets up and quickly walks out. *The police now reach the struggle, seize Thornhill and pull him to his feet.*

FIRST OFFICER
All right now . . .

THORNHILL
What took you so long?

SECOND OFFICER
(*pulling him towards the door*)
Let's take a little walk . . .

THORNHILL
Wait a minute . . .

SECOND OFFICER
Get moving.

THORNHILL
I haven't finished bidding yet . . .

FIRST OFFICER
(*dragging him along*)
Yeah, yeah.

THORNHILL
(*struggling*)
Three thousand! It's mine for three thousand!

Nearing the entrance they approach Valerian, standing there completely frustrated. Thornhill flashes him an apologetic smile as he is dragged by.

Sorry, old man. But keep trying.

Valerian watches without expression as Thornhill is escorted safely past him.

ANOTHER ANGLE
Thornhill and the two policemen continue through the lobby. Behind them is a telephone booth. We see the Professor standing beside it watching Thornhill being taken out. After they have passed him, the Professor glances after them briefly, then goes into the booth and closes the door.

EXT. SHAW & OPPENHEIM GALLERIES
The police emerge from the building with Thornhill and hurry him towards a patrol car parked at the curb.

THORNHILL
Handle with care, fellahs . . .

FIRST OFFICER
(*opening rear door*)
In there.

THORNHILL
. . . I'm valuable property.

FIRST OFFICER
In.

He pushes Thornhill into the car.

INT. PATROL CAR
Thornhill lands on the rear seat and the first officer joins him, while the other cop gets behind the wheel.

THORNHILL
I want to thank you boys for saving my life —

FIRST OFFICER
(*gruffly*)
Save it for the station-house.

The car starts away.

THORNHILL
(*buoyantly*)
Come on. Let's see some smiles and good cheer. You're about to become heroes. Know who I am?

FIRST OFFICER
(*disinterested*)
We'll find out as soon as we book ya for bein' drunk and disorderly.

THORNHILL
Drunk and disorderly? That's chicken feed. You've hit the *jackpot*, Sergeant . . .
(*as the Sergeant gives him a bored look*)
'Chicago police capture United Nations slayer.'

Now *the look is not so bored. Thornhill hands the half-believing sergeant his wallet saying:*

Roger Thornhill is the name. Take me to your leader.

While the Sergeant is quickly looking over Thornhill's identification cards, the Officer behind the wheel picks up a newspaper, glances at it, turns back to look at Thornhill and holds up the paper.

SECOND OFFICER
It's him!

In the back seat, the Sergeant leans forward, stares off-screen at the paper, then turns and looks at Thornhill.

THORNHILL
Congratulations, men.

FIRST OFFICER
(*awed*)

Yeah . . .

The man behind the wheel has taken up the telephone receiver on the dashboard and put in a call to headquarters. (The phone is similar to household instruments. We can hear only one end of the conversation.) During this, Thornhill sits back with smug expression.

SECOND OFFICER
(*to phone*)

This is one-oh-five-five. Sergeant Flamm. We got a man here answering to the description of Thornhill, Roger. Code seventy-six. Wanted by NYPD. Positive ID.
(*listens*)
Absolutely. No question.
(*listens*)
Michigan Avenue. Proceeding west to forty-second precinct.
(*listens*)
What?
(*listens*)
Come again?
(*listens*)
Ya sure?
(*listens*)
Okay.
(*listens*)
Right.
(*listens*)
Yeah. I got it.
(*listens*)
One-oh-five-five off and clear.

He hangs up, makes a swift U-turn and speeds off in the opposite direction.

FIRST OFFICER
(*startled*)

Where we goin'?

134

                    SECOND OFFICER
                        (*dejected*)
The airport.

                    FIRST OFFICER
For what?

                    SECOND OFFICER
                        (*disgusted*)
Orders.

                    THORNHILL
Just a second here. I'm not going to any airport. I want to be
taken to police headquarters.

                    SECOND OFFICER
Ya *do*, huh?

                    THORNHILL
                        (*leans forward*)
Why do you think I *sent* for you fellows?

                    SECOND OFFICER
How *about* this guy, Charley? He sent for us.

                    FIRST OFFICER
                        (*pulling Thornhill back*)
Sit back.

                    THORNHILL
Did you hear what I said? I want to be taken to police
headquarters! I'm a dangerous assassin! I'm a mad killer on
the loose!

                    SECOND OFFICER
You oughta be ashamed of yourself.

DISSOLVE TO:

EXT. MIDWAY AIRPORT, CHICAGO – NIGHT

*The police car pulls up, stops. The two Police Officers get out. Thornhill
gets out. They walk him into the terminal. In the background, the sound
of planes taking off.*

                            135

INT. NORTHWEST AIRLINES TERMINAL

They enter, and the police escort Thornhill to the Information Counter.

SECOND OFFICER
They said right here.

THORNHILL
(grumbling)
Does anybody mind if I sit down? I've been running all day.

Just then, the police see a man rushing through the door towards them. It is the Professor. He is breathless as he goes up to the Information Desk, giving Thornhill and the police a quick glance as he goes. We see the Professor lean over the desk and murmur something to the clerk, who nods, acknowledges him and immediately hands him an envelope of plane tickets. The clerk leans over his desk and points down the terminal building. The Professor turns and approaches the group, still out of breath. The camera moves into a closer angle. The Professor fumbles in his pockets, brings out an identification, which he shows to the police, all the while saying:

PROFESSOR
Never thought I'd make it. Getting too old for this kind of work.
(he glances at Thornhill)
All right. Thank you, men.
(takes Thornhill by the arm)
Let's go, Mr Thornhill. We haven't much time. This way is more private.

The following scene will be played in a fast-moving dolly shot as the Professor escorts Thornhill away from the police through the terminal, along a ramp, through a gate and across the field towards a waiting passenger plane. Movement will come to a halt only where indicated.

THORNHILL
I don't think I caught your name.

PROFESSOR
I don't think I pitched it.

THORNHILL

You're police, aren't you? Or is it FBI?

PROFESSOR

FBI . . . CIA . . . ONI . . . we're all in the same alphabet
soup.

THORNHILL

Well, put this in your alphabet soup: I had nothing to do with
that United Nations killing . . .

PROFESSOR

We know that.

THORNHILL
(*slows down*)

You do?

PROFESSOR
(*bumping a passerby*)

Sorry.

THORNHILL

Then what's the idea of the police chasing *me* all over the
map?

PROFESSOR

We never interfere with the police unless absolutely
necessary. It has become necessary.

THORNHILL

I take it, then, I'm to be cleared.

PROFESSOR
(*taking his arm*)

I do wish you'd walk faster, Mr Thornhill. We'll miss the
plane.

THORNHILL
(*walking faster*)

Where are we going – New York or Washington?

PROFESSOR

Rapid City, South Dakota.

THORNHILL
(*suspicious*)

Rapid City? What for?

PROFESSOR

It's near Mt Rushmore.

THORNHILL

I've already seen Mt Rushmore.

PROFESSOR

So has your friend Mr Vandamm.

THORNHILL
(*slowing down again*)

Vandamm?

PROFESSOR
(*wrily*)

A rather formidable gentleman, eh?

THORNHILL
(*with venom*)

And what about that treacherous tramp with him . . .

PROFESSOR

Miss Kendall?

THORNHILL

Yeah.

PROFESSOR

His mistress. We know all about her.

THORNHILL
(*bridling at this*)

What's Vandamm up to?

PROFESSOR
(*evasively*)

Let's say he's a kind of . . . importer-exporter.

THORNHILL

Of what?

PROFESSOR

Oh . . . you could say . . . government secrets perhaps?

THORNHILL

Why don't you grab him?

PROFESSOR

Too much we still don't know about his organization.

THORNHILL

Uh-huh. Well what's Mt Rushmore got to do with all this?

PROFESSOR

Vandamm has a place near there. We think it's his jumping-off point to leave the country tomorrow night.

THORNHILL

And you're going to stop him . . .

PROFESSOR

No.

THORNHILL
(*puzzled*)

Then . . . what are we *going* there for?

PROFESSOR

To set his mind at ease about George Kaplan.

Thornhill glances sharply at the Professor and peers at him for a moment.

THORNHILL

You, huh?

PROFESSOR

Eh?

THORNHILL
(*a statement*)

You're George Kaplan, *aren't* you . . .

PROFESSOR
(*blandly*)

Oh no, Mr Thornhill. There *is* no such person as George Kaplan.

Thornhill comes to a dead stop.

THORNHILL

Is no such person?

PROFESSOR

Come. We'll talk on the plane.

THORNHILL

But I've been in his hotel room! I've tried on his clothes! He's got short sleeves and . . . and dandruff!

PROFESSOR

Believe me, Mr Thornhill, he doesn't exist. Which is why I'm going to have to ask *you* to go on *being* him for another twenty-four hours.

Thornhill points a protesting finger at the Professor. Just as his mouth opens, there is the sudden roar of engines as a plane revs up and prepares to taxi away from the nearby ramp. Thornhill looks across at the plane with annoyance.

THE PLANE

As it starts to taxi away, its four engines creating a storm of noise and wind.

MEDIUM LONG SHOT: THORNHILL AND THE PROFESSOR

The two men are talking at each other, the Professor calmly, Thornhill gesticulating, arguing, denying, insisting, protesting. The Professor keeps tugging gently on Thornhill's arm, trying to move him along as he explains. As they start walking again, towards camera, they continue to talk to each other. We have heard none of this conversation, because distance from camera and the noise of the plane taxiing away have intervened . . . long enough for the Professor to give Thornhill a brief outline of the George Kaplan plan which we learned about in Washington. As the two men approach camera and walk through the gate on to the field, where another passenger plane stands waiting, the Professor appears to be making an appeal, and Thornhill is shaking his head vigorously. They have walked into a tighter two-shot and the sound of the taxiing plane has faded away. We can hear them now.

THORNHILL

Look – you started this crazy decoy business without me!
Finish it without me! . . .

PROFESSOR

And well we might have if you hadn't stumbled into it . . .

THORNHILL

. . . *I* think you should give me a *medal* and a *very* long *vacation*
instead of asking me to go *on* being a target just so that your
Number One, or whatever you call him, doesn't get shot at!

PROFESSOR

Not shot at, Mr Thornhill – *found out*. Once he's found out,
he's as good as dead. And thanks to *you* clouds of suspicion
are forming –

THORNHILL

Thanks to *me* – !

PROFESSOR

If you'll get on the plane –

THORNHILL

I'm an advertising man, not a red herring! I've got a job, a
secretary, a mother, two ex-wives and several bartenders
waiting for me, and I don't intend to disappoint them all and
get myself slightly killed by playing the man in the gray-
flannel cloak-and-dagger. The answer is no!

PROFESSOR

Is that final?

THORNHILL

Yes!

The Professor looks at him for a moment, then holds out his hand.

PROFESSOR

Goodbye then.
          (*as Thornhill takes the hand uncertainly*)
If I thought there was any chance of changing your mind, I'd
talk about Miss Kendall, whom you obviously disapprove of
for good reason . . .

141

THORNHILL
(*savagely*)
Yeah – for using sex like some people use a fly-swatter . . .
For trying to have me exterminated . . .

PROFESSOR
I don't suppose it would matter to you that she was probably
forced to do whatever she did . . . in order to protect herself.

THORNHILL
(*almost a sneer*)
Protect herself from *what*?

PROFESSOR
(*slowly*)
Suspicion . . . exposure . . . assassination.
(*Thornhill stares at him*)
Forgive me for referring to our Number One as a man, Mr
Thornhill. It's about all *I* can do to help keep her safe while
she's in all this terrible danger . . .

CLOSE SHOT: THORNHILL
*Turning to camera, eyes filled with emotion as he shakes his head
slowly, trying to throw off the pain of his confused feelings.*

PROFESSOR'S VOICE
(*off-screen*)
I know you didn't mean to, but I'm afraid you *have* put her in
a most delicate situation – and much more than her life is at
stake . . .

*During this, another plane has been arriving, its landing lights slowly
increasing the illumination on Thornhill's stricken face and the
background behind him. The sound of the engines rises, as though
illustrating the mounting determination within Thornhill, and his
ultimate decision.*

DISSOLVE TO:

LONG SHOT: THE PLANE IN FLIGHT – NIGHT

We are shooting up at the plane from an elevation on the ground as it approaches camera in a slightly descending path. As the plane comes nearer and zooms past, camera pans with it slightly and discovers:

THE FACES OF THE PRESIDENTS. MT RUSHMORE – NIGHT

The monument glows against the night sky, lit by several banks of unseen searchlights. We hold on this shot. And then the fading sound of the disappearing plane slowly becomes the sound of laughter and many voices. Slowly, night turns to day.

THE FACES OF THE PRESIDENTS – MT RUSHMORE – DAY

Same angle as above. The searchlights have been replaced by sunlight. The black sky has turned blue. Camera pulls back slowly, until a circular border appears at the edges of the screen. We are in:

EFFECT SHOT: THE FACES OF THE PRESIDENTS – AS SEEN THROUGH BINOCULARS

As soon as we have established the binocular effect –

    CUT TO:

CLOSE SHOT: THORNHILL – MT RUSHMORE OBSERVATION DECK

We are on Thornhill's back as he stands peering through binoculars mounted on a pedestal. (There are similar glasses located at many vantage points throughout the park.)

               THORNHILL
Suppose they don't come.

           PROFESSOR'S VOICE
              (off-screen)
They'll come.

During this we have pulled back to reveal the Professor sitting nearby reading a Rapid City newspaper, his back half-turned away from Thornhill.

               THORNHILL
              (uneasily)
I don't like the way Teddy Roosevelt is looking at me . . .

PROFESSOR
He's trying to give you one last word of caution, Mr Kaplan:
speak softly, and carry a big stick.

*Thornhill leaves the binoculars, starts restlessly past the Professor to the
corner of the terrace.*

THORNHILL
I think he's trying to tell me not to go through with this hair-
brained scheme . . .

PROFESSOR
Perhaps he doesn't know to what extent *you* are the *cause* of
our present difficulties –

THORNHILL
(*turning to him*)
I'm not so sure I *accept* that charge, Professor.

PROFESSOR
(*mildly*)
My dear fellow – if you had not made yourself so damnably
attractive to Miss Kendall that she fell for you –

THORNHILL
(*momentarily delighted*)
And vice versa.

PROFESSOR
– Our friend Vandamm wouldn't be losing faith in her loyalty
now. It was quite obvious to him last night that she had
become emotionally involved, worst of all with a man he
thinks is a government agent.

THORNHILL
Are you trying to tell me – *and* Teddy Roosevelt – that I'm
irresistible?

PROFESSOR
(*sternly*)
I'm trying to remind you that it's *your* responsibility to help us
restore her to Vandamm's good graces . . .
(*he sees Thornhill's face cloud over*)

144

. . . Right up to the moment he leaves the country tonight.

> THORNHILL
> (*annoyed*)

All right. All right.
(*he points a finger to remind the Professor of a previous bargain*)
But after tonight . . .

> PROFESSOR
> (*looking away*)

My blessings on you both.

Thornhill nods. Then he looks off-screen and reacts tensely.

> THORNHILL

Here they are.

The Professor's nonchalance vanishes instantly. He gets up and walks swiftly away. Thornhill looks off again.

POINT OF VIEW: THE PARKING AREA
A white Lincoln convertible is pulling into a parking space, comes to a stop. The driver is Vandamm. Eve and Leonard sit beside him. They get out of the car, glance about and start towards the cafeteria building.

THORNHILL
Watches them for a moment, then turns purposefully and hurries towards the cafeteria from his level. We move with him either with a dolly shot or a series of cuts, depending on the location of his starting point.

(It will not always be specifically indicated, but it should be borne in mind that the entire Mt Rushmore day sequence takes place with sightseers, camera bugs, little children and assorted tourists in evidence at all times, whether outdoors or indoors.)

EXT. MT RUSHMORE CAFETERIA & GIFT SHOP BUILDING

Thornhill approaches the building and enters.

INT. BUILDING – MASTER SCENE

Thornhill walks across the lobby to the cafeteria, a vast room with many tables and enormous windows through which can be seen the faces of the presidents in the distance. It is after the lunch hour, and only half of the tables are occupied. Thornhill goes over to the steam-table and asks for a cup of coffee. While waiting for it, he turns and looks towards the parking area entrance to the cafeteria. No one is coming through there yet. He receives the cup of coffee and starts towards an unoccupied table. Just as he arrives at the table, he sees Vandamm, Leonard and Eve enter the cafeteria. He remains standing until they see him. Then he sits down, as Vandamm and Eve walk towards him. Leonard sits down at a table near the entrance, as though he were a sentry standing guard in case of trouble.

AT THE TABLE
Vandamm and Eve arrive at the table. Eve has a strained look. Thornhill contemptuously refuses even to glance at her. His ignoring of her presence is his way of demonstrating to Vandamm how bitterly he despises her. (Thornhill is now playing a terse, matter-of-fact 'Kaplan' rather than his usual protesting self.)

> VANDAMM
> *(with a mild smile)*

Good afternoon, Mr Kaplan.

He starts to draw out a chair for Eve.

> THORNHILL
> *(sharply)*

Not her.

Vandamm's manner changes. He turns to Eve and, with a sharp incline of the head, dismisses her. Tight-lipped, Eve turns and walks off towards the gift shop. Thornhill looks after her with noticeable distaste. Vandamm sits down, resuming his deceptively polite manner.

(At times during the following, Thornhill will look past Vandamm towards the gift shop and we will see that Eve, 'browsing' in the gift shop, is standing right next to another 'browser', who could even be exchanging whispered words with her. It is the Professor. And if Leonard, seated near the doorway, would turn his head, he might even see them. But he does not turn his head. And he does not know the Professor.)

146

VANDAMM

Did I misunderstand you about bringing her?

THORNHILL

We'll get to that.

(*as he lights a cigarette*)

I suppose you were surprised to get my call . . .

VANDAMM

Not at all. I knew the police would release *you*, Mr Kaplan. By the way, I want to compliment you on your colorful exit from the auction gallery . . .

THORNHILL

Thank you.

VANDAMM

And now what little drama are we here for today? You see, I don't for a moment believe that you invited me to these gay surroundings in order to come to an arrangement . . .

THORNHILL

Suppose I were to tell you that I not only know exactly what time you're leaving the country tonight, but also the latitude and longitude of your rendezvous, and your ultimate destination.

VANDAMM

(*after a beat*)

You wouldn't care to carry my bags, would you?

THORNHILL

Maybe you'd like to know the price, just the same.

VANDAMM

Price?

THORNHILL

For doing nothing to stop you.

VANDAMM

(*amused*)

How much did you have in mind?

147

THORNHILL

I want the girl . . .

The geniality dies on Vandamm's face for a moment. Then he gives a little smile of understanding.

(shakes his head, then speaks with bitterness)
I want her to get what's coming to her. You turn her over to *me* and I'll see that there's enough pinned on *her* to keep her uncomfortable for the rest of her life. In return, I'll look the other way tonight.

Vandamm peers at him for a moment.

VANDAMM

She really got under your skin, didn't she?

THORNHILL
(angrily)
We're not talking about my skin. We're talking about yours. I'm offering you a chance to save it . . .

VANDAMM

To *exchange* it . . .

THORNHILL

Put it any way you like.

VANDAMM

I'm curious, Mr Kaplan. How did you arrive at this deduction that my feelings for Miss Kendall might have deteriorated to the point where I would . . . trade her in for . . . a little peace of mind?

THORNHILL

I don't deduce. I observe.

The two men stare at each other steadily. Then Vandamm looks up and gets to his feet.

FULL SHOT: THE TABLE
Eve is standing beside the table, her face tense. She doesn't look at Thornhill.

EVE
(*coldly*)
Phillip – if you don't mind, I'm going back to the house.

She immediately turns and starts to leave the cafeteria. Vandamm, momentarily caught off guard, looks after her hesitantly, and then, after a quick look at Thornhill, goes after her.

CLOSE-UP: THORNHILL
Looking off after them. He rises with concern on his face.

POINT OF VIEW: FROM THORNHILL
Vandamm has caught up with Eve. There is a brief unheard exchange between them, then Vandamm beckons Leonard over to them and the three start swiftly towards the exit.

CLOSE SHOT: THORNHILL
Seeing this turn of events and reacting to it, he starts after them.

WIDER ANGLE (MASTER SCENE)
Thornhill moves swiftly across the cafeteria to head off Vandamm, Eve and Leonard, who are approaching the door leading out to the parking area. Thornhill catches up with Eve, puts a hand on her.

THORNHILL
(*quietly and tensely*)
Just a second, you.

Vandamm and Leonard, a few steps ahead of her, stop and look back.

EVE
(*mutters, pulling free*)
Get away from me!

She goes towards the two men, who are starting to return. Thornhill grabs Eve by the arm, pulls her, struggling, back into the cafeteria.

(*through her breath*)
Let go!

Vandamm starts to make a move towards the struggling Eve and Thornhill. Leonard quickly stays him. All of this takes place with lightning rapidity. Vandamm watches tensely.

149

Let *go* of me!

THORNHILL

You're not going anywhere . . .
> (*he pulls her violently away from the others*)

Come on . . .

The camera moves in for a close-up of Vandamm. From his point of view, we see the struggling couple.

EVE

No! . . . Please! . . .

THORNHILL

Save the phoney tears . . .

She breaks out of his grasp, backs away. He comes towards her, stops suddenly. She has taken her automatic from her handbag, points it at him.

EVE

Get back . . .

THORNHILL

You little fool . . .

He starts slowly towards her. She backs towards the entrance, eyes wide with terror.

EVE

Stay away from me . . .

Thornhill lunges at her. She fires at him once. He clutches his chest, stops dead in his tracks. She fires again. He spins, crashes into a table and falls to the floor. Crowds scream. Pandemonium ensues. Eve dashes out past Vandamm, who starts to follow, but Leonard restrains him.

LEONARD

No good, sir. You can't get involved in this.

IN A SERIES OF QUICK CUTS:

1 The Professor is seen running across the cafeteria towards Thornhill's fallen body.

2 Eve is seen running down the path towards the parking area.

3 Leonard is seen unobtrusively escorting Vandamm to the back of the crowd.

4 The Professor is seen pushing his way through the crowds surrounding Thornhill's body, saying: 'Get back! Please! Don't touch anything!'

5 Eve is seen getting into Vandamm's car, gunning the motor, speeding away.

6 Leonard is seen moving up to the edge of the crowd surrounding Thornhill's body, maneuvering himself into position until he can see:

7 The Professor kneeling over Thornhill's body, feeling the heart. He withdraws his hands, wipes blood from his fingers with a handkerchief and looks up gravely as a shocked murmur arises from the onlookers and one woman begins to cry.

QUICK DISSOLVE TO:

EXT. DRIVEWAY ENTRANCE TO PARK — FEW MINUTES LATER

Shooting over the heads of hushed onlookers in foreground, we see two green-uniformed park attendants bearing Thornhill on a stretcher to the rear of a parked hospital van. Several men remove their hats as the *stretcher goes by. The Professor is on hand to supervise as the stretcher is placed in the van and the rear doors are shut. Now the Professor gets in the front seat beside the driver, and the van drives off.*

QUICK DISSOLVE TO:

EXT. SECLUDED ROAD – A FEW MINUTES LATER

Camera is on a lovely wooded glen securely hidden from the main road that cuts through the Black Hills. Perhaps the Mt Rushmore monument can be seen in the distance through the trees. Camera pans over, revealing the parked ambulance. The Professor is in the act of opening the back doors. He peers in.

> PROFESSOR

Mr Thornhill . . .

Thornhill rises with alacrity.

> THORNHILL

Are we there?

> PROFESSOR

No.

Thornhill looks off, sees someone and slides out of the ambulance to his feet. He stands for a moment looking off. Then, as he starts slowly forward, camera eases back ultimately to reveal Eve standing beside the white Lincoln convertible. During this, the Professor has started back towards the front of the ambulance, saying:

Don't be long.

Thornhill and Eve regard each other uncertainly as she starts moving towards him. Camera now eases in, ultimately to a two shot.

They continue to gaze at each other uncertainly. In a way, they are meeting for the first time, for it is the first time that they are together with Thornhill knowing who Eve is and with Eve aware that Thornhill knows who she is. (The play-acting scene at the cafeteria did not count, for they were prevented from acknowledging the true situation.) After all that Eve has done to Thornhill and he has said to her, neither can be certain of the other's true feelings. It is a time for uneasiness, caution and tentative probing – eventually giving way

152

to what has always been apparent: the fact that they do like each other more than somewhat.

EVE

Hello . . .

THORNHILL

Hello . . .

A moment of silence.

EVE

Are you all right?

THORNHILL

Yes. I think so.

More silence. They move closer.

EVE

I asked the Professor to let me see you again . . .

THORNHILL

Oh?

He waits.

EVE

There isn't . . . much time . . .

THORNHILL
(non-committal)

Isn't there?

EVE

I . . . wanted to tell you . . . I mean . . . apologize . . .

THORNHILL
(without feeling)

No need. I understand . . .
(slightly bitter)
All in the line of duty . . .

EVE

I did treat you miserably . . .

153

THORNHILL
(*a self-accusation*)
I hated you for it . . .

EVE
(*faltering*)
And I didn't want you to . . . go on . . . thinking . . .

THORNHILL
(*softening slightly*)
I used some pretty harsh words. I'm . . . sorry . . .

EVE
They hurt . . . deeply . . .

THORNHILL
(*defensively*)
Naturally, if I'd known . . .

EVE
(*defensively*)
I couldn't tell you . . .

THORNHILL
No . . .

EVE
Could I?

THORNHILL
Of course not.

Eve gives the tiniest of shrugs. They gaze at each other. That is the whole situation. Nobody to blame really. No need for further apologies. They each were unkind to the other – but always with due cause. But mixed in with the unkind acts and harsh words had been other acts, other words, other feelings – no? Eve smiles at him tenderly.

EVE
You didn't get hurt. I'm so relieved.

THORNHILL
(*eagerly*)
Of course I was hurt. How would *you* have felt if – ?

154

                              EVE
I mean when you fell in the cafeteria, when I – bang bang –
shot you.

                           THORNHILL
                            (*smiles*)
Oh, that . . . No.

                              EVE
                        (*moving closer*)
You did it rather well, I thought.

                           THORNHILL
                      (*pleased with himself*)
Yes – I was quite . . . graceful . . .

                              EVE
                     (*putting her hands on him*)
Considering that it's not really your kind of work . . .

                           THORNHILL
                      (*touching her tenderly*)
I got into it by accident. What's *your* excuse?

                              EVE
I met Phillip Vandamm at a party one night and saw only his
charm. I guess I had nothing to do that weekend, so I decided
to fall in love . . .

                           THORNHILL
                 (*sorry he brought the whole thing up*)
That's nice.

                              EVE
Eventually, the Professor and his Washington colleagues
approached me with a few sordid details about Phillip and
told me that my . . . *relationship* with him made me 'uniquely
valuable' to them.

                           THORNHILL
                           (*bridling*)
So *you* turned Girl Scout.

                    EVE

Maybe it was the first time anyone ever asked me to do
anything worthwhile.

                THORNHILL

Has life been like that?

                    EVE

Mm hmmm.

                THORNHILL

How come?

                    EVE

Men like you.

                THORNHILL
                (*kissing her*)

What's wrong with men like me?

                    EVE

They don't believe in marriage.

                THORNHILL

I've been married twice.

                    EVE

See what I mean?

He looks at her with affection.

                THORNHILL

Y'know something. I may go back to hating you again. It was
more fun.

                    EVE
            (*with a trace of sadness*)

You're not going to have the chance. There isn't time.
            (*she gives him a quick embrace*)

Goodbye, Thornhill.

                THORNHILL
                (*holding her*)

Wait a minute. Not so soon.

EVE

I have to get back to the house and convince them I took the long way around so nobody would follow me there.

THORNHILL
(*holding her even closer*)
Can't we just stand like this for a few more hours?

EVE

You're supposed to be critically wounded.

THORNHILL

I never felt more alive.

EVE

Whose side are you on?

THORNHILL

Yours, always.

EVE

Then don't undermine my resolve, just when I need it most.

They hear the short beep of a horn and look off. The Professor is motioning to Thornhill to come.

THORNHILL

I guess it's off to the hospital for *me* . . .
(*they start walking slowly*)
. . . And back to danger for you. I don't like it one bit.

EVE

Much safer now, thanks to you, my darling decoy.

THORNHILL

Don't thank me. I couldn't stand it.

EVE

All right. I won't.

THORNHILL

And just as soon as your malevolent friend Vandamm takes off tonight, I'm going to undo my bandages, and you and I are going to do a lot of apologizing to each other, in private . . .

EVE
(*glancing at him wistfully*)
Don't talk like that . . .

THORNHILL
It's the way I feel . . .

EVE
You mustn't . . .

THORNHILL
I must . . .

EVE
You know it can't be.

THORNHILL
(*unconcerned*)
Of course it can be.

Eve stops, looks up at him, disturbed. She glances towards the Professor.

EVE
He *has* told you, hasn't he?

THORNHILL
(*puzzled*)
Told me what?

Eve shakes her head, unable to speak.

PROFESSOR
(*coming up to them*)
Miss Kendall – you've *got* to get moving . . .

EVE
(*with a final embrace*)
Goodbye, Thornhill . . .

THORNHILL
(*holding on to her*)
Wait a minute . . .
(*to the Professor*)
What didn't you tell me?

Eve and the Professor glance at each other. There are tears in Eve's eyes now.

EVE

Why didn't you?

For a brief moment, the Professor's face reveals an all-too-human regret for what he has done. Then he looks at Thornhill and speaks crisply.

PROFESSOR

She's going off with Vandamm tonight on the plane.

THORNHILL
(*stunned*)

Going off with Vandamm?

PROFESSOR

That's why we've gone to such lengths to make her a fugitive from justice – so that Vandamm couldn't very well decline to take her along –

THORNHILL

But you said –

PROFESSOR

I needn't tell you how valuable she can be to us over there.

THORNHILL

You lied to me! You said after tonight – !

PROFESSOR

I needed your help . . .

THORNHILL
(*bitterly*)

Well, *you got* it all right . . .

EVE
(*through tears*)

Don't be angry . . .

THORNHILL
(*to Eve*)

If you think I'm going to let you go through with this dirty business – !

159

She has to.

THORNHILL
(*turning on him*)
Nobody has to do anything! I don't like the games you play,
Professor – !

PROFESSOR
War is hell, Mr Thornhill – even when it's a cold one.

THORNHILL
(*savagely*)
– If you fellows can't lick the Vandamms without asking girls
like her to bed down with them and fly away with them and
probably never come back alive, maybe you better start
learning to *lose* a few cold wars!

PROFESSOR
(*quietly*)
I'm afraid we're already doing that.

*Suddenly Eve breaks away, runs for her car. Thornhill goes after her,
and the Professor quickly motions to the ambulance driver to step down.*

AT THE CAR
*Eve gets into the car, starts the motor, as Thornhill catches up with her
and pulls open the door to stop her.*

THORNHILL
I'm not going to let you . . .

EVE
Don't spoil everything now . . . please . . .

THORNHILL
Come on – *out* . . .

A hand taps him on the back. He turns.

CLOSE SHOT: THE AMBULANCE DRIVER
*His fist is cocked, and moving on the backward arc of a knockout
punch.*

CUT TO:

CLOSE SHOT: THE CAR DOOR
Slamming shut as though it were illustrating the impact of fist on jaw. The car drives off with a screech of tires, and we see Thornhill falling into the shot, and to the ground.

DISSOLVE TO:

INT. HOSPITAL ROOM – NIGHT

Start close on a bedside radio. During broadcast pull back to reveal Thornhill in trousers and undershirt. His jacket, tie and red-stained shirt hang nearby. He is pacing back and forth, nervously smoking a cigarette.

RADIO ANNOUNCER'S VOICE
– in full view of scores of horrified men, women and children who had come to the park to see the famed Mt Rushmore monument. Witnesses to the shooting described Kaplan's assailant as an attractive blonde in her late twenties. Kaplan, who was removed to the Rapid City Hospital in critical condition, has been tentatively identified as an employee of the Federal Government . . . The tragedy developed with startling suddenness. Chris Swenson, a busboy in the Mt Rushmore cafeteria, stated that he heard voices raised in what seemed to be –

Thornhill angrily switches off the radio and snuffs out his cigarette in an ashtray with a violent thrust. He goes to the single window which is open, stares down at the street many stories below. He turns, walks towards the door, feeling his jaw and wincing with pain. He pulls at the doorknob, knowing it is locked but unable to resist giving it another try. Impatiently he hits at the unyielding door as though it were his enemy. He is locked in, and quite obviously he'd like to be out. He begins to pace the room again. Now he hears footsteps approaching in the hallway outside, then a key in the lock. Quickly, and with noticeable cunning, he lies down on the bed. The door opens and the Professor walks in carrying a brand-new white shirt.

PROFESSOR
(*handing him the shirt*)
Here we are. Sixteen and three-quarter collar, thirty-five
sleeves, no ketchup stains.

THORNHILL
Thanks.

He starts to put on the shirt.

PROFESSOR
How are you feeling?

THORNHILL
All right – considering that your driver was born with a
sledgehammer instead of a hand.

PROFESSOR
Sorry about that.

THORNHILL
(*pretending*)
No. I deserved it.
(*gesturing towards the door*)
And that locked door too . . .

PROFESSOR
If you were seen wandering about in good health, it could
prove fatal to Miss Kendall . . .

THORNHILL
No need to lock me in anymore.

PROFESSOR
Good.

THORNHILL
I've been acting childish . . .

*Thornhill turns away from the Professor and we see on his face that he
has ulterior motives.*

PROFESSOR
We all do at times, where a woman is concerned.

THORNHILL

I've already started to forget her.

PROFESSOR

Good . . .

THORNHILL

Yes.

PROFESSOR

Better that way.

THORNHILL

Much.

PROFESSOR

Inside of an hour she'll be gone.

Thornhill has to tighten his lips to keep from showing anything to the Professor other than utter lack of interest.

THORNHILL

How goes it in the world outside?

PROFESSOR

Fine. Mr Kaplan's untimely shooting has now acquired the authority of the printed word. Enormous headlines. Everyone has been cooperating beautifully.

THORNHILL

You may now include *me*.

PROFESSOR

I'm most grateful.

THORNHILL

A favor in return?

PROFESSOR

Anything.

THORNHILL

A bottle of scotch. A pint'll do.

PROFESSOR

May I join you?

THORNHILL

Wonderful. Make it a quart.

The Professor goes to the door, opens it and looks back.

PROFESSOR

See you in a few minutes.

Thornhill smiles, the picture of friendly cooperation. The door closes softly. And almost before it has clicked shut, Thornhill's smile disappears. He seizes his jacket, struggles into it, closes his collar at the neck, stuffs his tie into his pocket and steps to the door. He turns the knob and pulls. To his surprise and dismay, the door is locked. The Professor has been one step ahead of him.

THORNHILL
(*with disgust*)

Why, the dirty sneak.

He looks around, glances at his wrist-watch, makes a decision, goes to the window and looks down at the street below. Then he takes a deep breath, swallows his fear and climbs out onto the ledge.

THE LEDGE

Thornhill inches his way along the shallow ledge until he comes to another window, partially open. He raises it as silently as he can and starts to climb in.

INT. ANOTHER HOSPITAL ROOM

The room is in darkness. Thornhill's silhouette is framed in the window as he climbs in. As his feet touch the floor, a light suddenly comes on. An attractive Brunette has switched on the lamp on the night-table and now sits up in bed. Thornhill holds a finger to his lips, starts towards the bed (and the door beyond).

BRUNETTE

Stop!

THORNHILL
(*softly, as he walks by*)

Excuse me.

The woman quickly takes her harlequin glasses from the night-table, puts them on and looks at Thornhill as he goes past the bed and continues on to the door.

> BRUNETTE
> *(in an entirely different tone of voice)*
> Stop . . .

Thornhill opens the door and walks out on the invitation.

DISSOLVE TO:

EXT. ROAD BEYOND MT RUSHMORE — NIGHT

A taxi is speeding along a winding dirt road.

ANOTHER ANGLE
The cab slows down and comes to a stop near the beginning of a high stone wall.

CLOSER SHOT
As Thornhill gets out of the cab, the driver turns to him.

> DRIVER
> Sure you don't want me to take you right up there?

> THORNHILL
> No. This is fine.

The cab drives off.

THORNHILL
He looks about, then moves along the wall until he comes to a pair of heavy iron gates — the only entrance to the area beyond the wall. The gates are open. He goes through and sees:

ESTABLISHING SHOT: VANDAMM'S HOUSE
It is a sprawling modern structure in the Frank Lloyd Wright tradition set on a rise in the land at the end of a long driveway. Lights are ablaze. There is evidence of activity within.

ANOTHER ANGLE: WITH THORNHILL

Cautiously he approaches the house and makes his way around to the back. The terrain there is rocky and slopes sharply down to a level field. The house juts out over this slope, cantilever style. As Thornhill stands in the dark looking about, he suddenly sees:

THE FIELD BEHIND THE HOUSE

Two parallel rows of lights several hundred yards long. They are very clearly the runway lights of a hidden landing strip. They flash off and on again, as though being tested, and then the field falls back into darkness.

ANOTHER ANGLE: WITH THORNHILL

He turns around and starts up the slope, moving to his right towards the side of the house where the incline is less steep. Just as he reaches the house, he stops, on the alert, as he hears the sound of an approaching car. He looks off, sees:

POINT OF VIEW

The headlights of the approaching car sweep along the driveway, and then the car itself is seen coming around the side of the house and pulling to a stop in the parking area. It is a small sedan. The driver gets out. It is Valerian. He is carrying a newspaper. At this moment, a side door of the house opens and a woman walks out to meet Valerian. It is the housekeeper last seen at the Townsend estate in Glen Cove. Together, they go towards the house, moving directly towards Thornhill.

THORNHILL

He quickly ducks beneath the cantilevered portion of the house and hides. He hears a door opening and closing, then footsteps and voices inside the house above him, the sound coming through the floor. Thornhill glances about, then decides to climb up one of the cantilevers. This will enable him to get a view of what might be going on inside the house. All the time that he has been underneath the house, he has been hearing a mumble of voices from above. He moves forward.

ANOTHER ANGLE: EXT. HOUSE

Thornhill appears from beneath the house, groping his way up the diagonal beam of the cantilever and then climbing up onto the

*horizontal beam. He is now outside one of the large windows of the
living-room. A section of the window is open. With cat-like stealth he
moves along the cantilever towards the window, takes up a position in
the shadows and peers inside.*

INT. LIVING-ROOM – FROM THORNHILL

*A large room, strikingly furnished, and dominated by a great chandelier
which hangs suspended from the two-story-high beamed ceiling. A
stairway at the far end leads to a balcony which runs the length of the
room. Off this balcony are bedrooms. In foreground near the window is
a table on which can be seen some effects of Vandamm – a black
briefcase, books strapped together, boxes of his favorite cigarettes, and
the pre-Columbian figure, the Tarascan warrior, purchased at the
auction. Vandamm and Eve are near the bar. Close to them is an
opened newspaper. Eve appears strained. (Her parting with Thornhill
has threatened her self-control considerably.) Vandamm, assuming that
she is upset over the shooting, has been trying to comfort her in a
soothing, gentle voice.*

VANDAMM

– Nothing to worry about –

EVE

– I lost my head –

*During following, Leonard enters in background unobserved by them.
He watches them with a curious smirk on his face, as though he were in
possession of a delightful secret unknown to anyone but him.*

VANDAMM

I'm not just saying this to make you feel better, my dear. I
mean it . . .

EVE

I didn't know what I was doing . . .

VANDAMM

He was going to destroy you. You had to protect yourself . . .

EVE

But not endanger *you* . . .

167

VANDAMM

Nonsense. There's not a word, not a whisper that links you or me, *any* of us, with this thing. There would have been *some* hint on the radio or in the paper. Look for yourself.

EVE
(*shaking her head*)
I don't want to look . . .

VANDAMM
(*with sympathy*)
Or even think about it. I can understand that.
(*he takes her face in his hands*)
Will you ever forgive me, my dear?

EVE

Forgive you?

VANDAMM

For upsetting you so . . . for not showing more confidence in your devotion . . .

EVE
(*a wan smile*)
Dear Phillip . . .

VANDAMM

Soon we'll be off together, and I shall dedicate myself to your happiness.

He kisses her gently, then turns towards Leonard.

What's the situation, Leonard?

LEONARD
(*facetiously*)
About the plane, you mean?

VANDAMM

Of course. What was the last report?

LEONARD

Over Whitestone on the hour. Six thousand. Descending.

VANDAMM

Another ten minutes.

LEONARD

At the most.

VANDAMM

Bags?

LEONARD

Outside.

VANDAMM

Runway lights?

LEONARD

Checked.

VANDAMM

Good.

LEONARD

And now, I wonder if I could have a few words of parting
with you, sir?

VANDAMM

Certainly.

LEONARD
(*looking at Eve*)

In private?

Vandamm glances sharply at Leonard. Eve senses tension, quickly relieves the situation.

EVE

I'll go upstairs and get my things.

She starts up the stairs.

OUTSIDE THE WINDOW
Thornhill watches as Eve goes up to the balcony. Leonard stares at her all the way, and Vandamm peers at him, *sensing hostility in his attitude. When Eve disappears into one of the bedrooms, Vandamm addresses Leonard with a trace of facetiousness.*

VANDAMM

Well, Leonard – how does one say farewell to one's own right arm?

LEONARD

In your case, sir, I'm afraid you're going to wish you had cut it off sooner . . .

During the above interchange, Thornhill will glance sharply up to his right when he sees the lights go on in the balcony bedroom window, and then Eve herself appear for a moment at the window. The voices in the living-room dwindle to an unintelligible drone *as Thornhill backs away from the open living-room window towards the end of the cantilever beam. He is now in a better position to attract Eve's attention. He glances about for a pebble to throw, but he is too far above ground to reach one. He takes a coin from his pocket, glances cautiously towards the living-room, then looks up and throws the coin at Eve's window. It hits noisily and falls to the ground below.*

INTERCUT SEVERAL ANGLES
Eve appears at the window, looks out for a moment, then walks away.

Thornhill takes another coin from his pocket, throws it at the window and hits again.

Eve appears at the window, opens it and looks out.

Just as Thornhill starts to call to her, he glances sharply towards the living-room.

Leonard is walking briskly over to the open living-room window. In a moment he will see Thornhill.

Thornhill ducks back into the shadows against the house.

Leonard peers out of the living-room window to see the cause of the noise he had heard; Eve continues to look out of the bedroom window. Thornhill cannot move out to signal her. Seeing nothing, Eve closes the window again and walks away.

Thornhill glances towards the living-room window and his eyes widen:

Leonard has moved away from the window and, with his back to Vandamm, is taking a gun from his pocket and placing it on a table near the window, as Vandamm talks in background, his words unintelligible.

Thornhill edges up to the window, as Leonard turns around, the gun concealed on the table behind him. The dialogue becomes intelligible again.

INTERCUT INT. LIVING-ROOM & CLOSE-UPS OF THORNHILL LISTENING

> LEONARD
> You must have had *some* doubts about her yourself, and *still do* —

> VANDAMM
> (*disturbed, and trying to conceal it*)
> Rubbish . . .

> LEONARD
> — Why else would you have decided not to tell her that our little treasure here . . .
> (*patting the figure of the Tarascan warrior*)

171

. . . has a bellyfull of microfilm?

VANDAMM
(*angrily*)
You seem to be trying to fill *mine* with rotten apples.

LEONARD
Sometimes the truth does taste like a mouthful of worms, sir.

VANDAMM
(*snorts*)
What truth? I've heard nothing but innuendoes.

LEONARD
Call it my woman's intuition if you will, but I've never trusted
neatness. Neatness is always the result of deliberate planning.

VANDAMM
(*defensively*)
She shot him in a moment of fear and anger. You were there.
You saw it.

LEONARD
(*nods*)
And thereby wrapped everything up into one very neat and
tidy bundle:

*During the preceding speech, he picks up the gun, holds it behind his
back and advances further into the room, the camera following through
the window.*

A. She removed any doubts you might have had about – what
did you call it? – her *'devotion'* and B. She gave herself a new
and *urgent* reason to be taken over to the other side with you,
just in *case* you decided to change your mind.

Vandamm manages a laugh, but it is not very convincing.

VANDAMM
You know what *I* think? I think you're jealous of her. I mean
it. And I'm touched, dear boy. Really touched.

*Suddenly Leonard brings the gun out from behind his back and points it
at the startled Vandamm.*
(*sharply*)
Leonard!

*Leonard pulls the trigger, fires point blank at Vandamm. There is a
sharp report. Vandamm stands there, stunned but unharmed.*

LEONARD
(*softly*)
The gun she shot Kaplan with. I found it in her luggage.

WAIST SHOT: VANDAMM
*The camera is very high, looking down on him. As the full realization of
what this means sinks in, the camera slowly descends to examine his
expression, and the angle becomes a big head. Vandamm's reaction is
carefully controlled. He is too big a man to let Leonard see the
humiliation and anger he feels at having been duped by Eve.*

LEONARD'S VOICE
(*during above*)
It's an old Gestapo trick. Shoot one of your own people to

show that you're not one of them. They've just freshened it up a bit with blank cartridges.

Vandamm gives a little sigh.

>   VANDAMM
> What a pity . . .

From upstairs, the sound of a door opening. Vandamm looks up, and his brooding expression quickly changes to a wistful smile.

> Ready, dear?

CLOSE SHOT: EVE
Standing at the balcony railing looking down at him.

>   EVE
> I thought I heard a shot . . .

FULL SHOT: THE LIVING-ROOM

>   VANDAMM
>   (*calmly*)
> Yes . . . so did we . . .
>   (*moves towards the window*)
> Must have been a car backfiring or something.
>   (*looks out*)
> Hurry down, pet. Almost time to go.

>   EVE
> In a moment.

She goes back into her room. Leonard moves at Vandamm, speaking in a harsh voice.

>   LEONARD
> You're not taking her on that plane with you?

>   VANDAMM
> Of course I am.

Leonard stares at him. Vandamm looks back at him the way an adult looks at a small boy.

> Like our friends, I too believe in neatness, Leonard.

                              (*a pause*)
This matter is best disposed of from a great height . . . over
water.

CLOSE SHOT: THORNHILL
Aghast at what he has heard.

WIDER ANGLE
*Thornhill backs away from the open window, looks up at Eve's
bedroom. The light is still on. Inside the living-room, Valerian has
entered in background and is receiving instructions from Vandamm.
Leonard has taken up a position near the open window. Even if he
thought it would do any good, Thornhill would not dare hurl another
coin at Eve's window now. His lips tighten. He makes a decision, starts
to climb up the side of the house to her room.*

CLOSE ANGLE: THORNHILL
*The camera follows him as he makes his way precariously up the side of
the house. Eve's window is beyond him and always in view. We see her
moving about and putting on her things during his climb. There is little
on which Thornhill can gain purchase as he climbs, little to hang on to.
He cuts his hand. Several times he almost crashes to disaster. The last
few feet are the hardest. He claws his way to the window sill of Eve's
bedroom, grabs it with his left hand, pulls himself up, gets his right hand
working, and with a final gasp, gets his body up high enough to be able
to see through the closed window into the room. Just as his head clears
the sill, the lights in the room go out and, over his shoulder, we see Eve
silhouetted in the doorway, walking out.*

INT. BEDROOM

*Thornhill, outside the window, stares dejectedly through the glass, then
silently works the window open. He climbs into the room and stands
there for a moment in the semi-darkness catching his breath. He looks at
his cut hand, takes out his handkerchief and presses it into the bleeding
palm. Then he steps cautiously to the doorway and looks out over the
living-room below. He cannot see much of the room because of the
balcony, and his unfavorable vantage point. But he can hear voices:*

VANDAMM'S VOICE

How about a little champagne before we go?

EVE'S VOICE

I'd love it.

VANDAMM'S VOICE

(*after he walks to bar*)

It may not be cold enough.

EVE'S VOICE

Over the rocks will be all right.

VANDAMM'S VOICE

Really?

EVE'S VOICE

Sure.

VANDAMM'S VOICE

Good idea.

Suddenly Thornhill glances back towards the open window, alarmed at what he hears – the first faint drone of an approaching plane. He looks about desperately, not knowing what to do. His eyes fall on the handkerchief still held in his hand. He sees his monogram: 'ROT' on the cloth. He glances towards the doorway, and an idea is born. He feels in his side pocket and takes out a match folder. (In an insert, we see that the match folder is the same one he and Eve discussed at dinner on the train. It bears his personal trademark: ROT.) *He takes a pen from his pocket, opens the match folder and writes a message on the inside of the cover:* 'THEY'RE ON TO YOU! COME UP TO YOUR ROOM!' *He closes the folder, goes to the doorway and moves cautiously out to the balcony.*

HIGH ANGLE

Shooting down over Thornhill in foreground as he edges forwards on the balcony, we see more of the living-room below. Eve is seated on the arm of a sofa. Her handbag is on the coffee table. Vandamm is turning away from the bar, walking towards her with a glass of champagne on the rocks in each hand. He gives her one, and they click glasses.

VANDAMM

To you, my dear . . . and all the lovely moments we've had together . . .

EVE

Thank you, Phillip.

As they drink, Leonard enters, walks towards the window.

LEONARD

He's circling.

Vandamm turns away from Eve, starts towards Leonard and the window. At this, Thornhill tosses the folder of matches down at Eve. Just as he does so, she takes a sip of champagne and fails to see the folder land on the floor nearby.

LOW ANGLE: IN LIVING-ROOM

VANDAMM
(*to Leonard*)

Jump in. The champagne is fine.

LEONARD

There isn't time.

VANDAMM
(*ruefully*)

You always *were* a spoilsport, weren't you?

LEONARD
(*starting past him towards Eve*)

One of my most valuable attributes, as it now turns out.

Automatically he stoops down and picks up the match folder lying on the floor, playing with it idly as he addresses Eve. (Thornhill watches in agony.)

It would please me if you would think of me as being along on this journey, if only in spirit . . .

EVE

I shall, Leonard . . .

177

Leonard tosses the match folder to the coffee table before her and turns away, so that she cannot see his harsh expression. Eve sets her glass down on the coffee table as the sound of the plane grows louder. And then she sees the match folder.

CLOSE-UP: EVE
For a moment she is puzzled. Then her glance goes to the floor where she had seen Leonard pick up the matches. Realization begins to dawn on her.

> VANDAMM'S VOICE
> *(off-screen)*

Come along, Eve.

> EVE

All right . . .

She gets to her feet, takes a cigarette from the coffee table, puts it between her lips and takes up the matches. We are very close as she opens the folder and reads Thornhill's message *while striking a match and lighting the cigarette.*

ANOTHER ANGLE
She looks up, sees the two men standing there waiting for her. She starts towards them, then suddenly feels her ear.

> EVE

Oh, I think I left my earrings upstairs . . .

Before they can say anything, she runs right past them and up the stairs, clutching the match folder tightly.

Be right down.

Vandamm and Leonard glance at each other, then look towards her as she goes upstairs.

POINT OF VIEW: FROM MEN
Eve going up the stairs and along the balcony to her room.

CLOSE SHOT: VANDAMM AND LEONARD
Watching her.

INT. BEDROOM

Thornhill draws back into the bedroom as he sees Eve coming. She runs into the room, snaps on the light. He grabs her and pulls her towards the window as they speak in very fast, urgent whispers.

> THORNHILL
>
> Quick! We can make it through the window! There's a car downstairs!

> EVE
> *(struggling)*
>
> Get away from here, you *idiot*! You'll ruin everything!

> THORNHILL
>
> Ruin everything? They know all about the fake shooting! They're going to do away with you!

> EVE
>
> What're you talking about?

> THORNHILL
>
> Leonard found the gun in your luggage! *You* heard the shot! . . .

Eve stares at him, then glances quickly towards the door as she hears footsteps on the stairs.

> . . . And I heard them say the figure they bought at the auction last night is filled with microfilm!

Eve turns, looks at Thornhill.

> EVE
>
> So that's how he's been getting the information.

> LEONARD'S VOICE
> *(from balcony)*
>
> Miss Kendall?

She breaks away and goes quickly towards the door.

> THORNHILL
> *(calling after her)*
>
> Don't get on that plane! I'll get the car!

She snaps off the light and hurries out to:

THE BALCONY
– Just in time to head off Leonard, who has reached the top of the stairs.
She closes the bedroom door behind her and goes quickly towards him.
He stops, waits for her and they both start down the stairs.

THE LIVING-ROOM
As Eve and Leonard descend the stairs, Vandamm is talking in a
reassuring tone of voice to the Housekeeper, who appears troubled.

> VANDAMM
> Don't worry, Anna. Arrangements have been made. You and
> your husband will be over the Canadian border by morning.

> HOUSEKEEPER
> Thank you, sir.

> VANDAMM
> Be careful now.

> HOUSEKEEPER
> We will, sir. And God bless you.

Vandamm turns and picks up the pre-Columbian figure while Leonard
crosses over and picks up the briefcase, the books and the cigarettes.
Eve's glance is on the figure held by Vandamm as he comes over
to her. *The three of them now start out through the exit door under the*
stairs as the Housekeeper starts up the room. As the Housekeeper goes
out of the picture we see the balcony bedroom door open and Thornhill
cautiously stepping forward and looking out.

POINT OF VIEW
The Housekeeper is retreating towards the other end of the room.

CLOSE SHOT: THE HOUSEKEEPER
Her walk slows up as she sees:

INSERT: A TURNED OFF TELEVISION SET
It reflects Thornhill standing on the distant balcony behind her.

CLOSE SHOT: PROFILE OF HOUSEKEEPER
She is still walking slowly. She turns her head ever so slightly, conscious of Thornhill's presence, and then makes her way around a corner out of sight.

CLOSE SHOT: THORNHILL
Satisfied that the woman is gone, he goes quickly along the balcony and down the stairs, camera following. As he reaches the bottom step, he hears:

> HOUSEKEEPER'S VOICE
> Stay where you are!

Thornhill turns, startled and sees:

POINT OF VIEW
The Housekeeper slowly advancing towards him from the far end of the room. She is holding a gun, pointed at him.

WIDER ANGLE
She stops within a few yards of him, motions towards a nearby chair.

> HOUSEKEEPER
> Sit down.
> *(Thornhill sits)*
> As soon as the plane leaves, Mr Leonard and my husband will be back.

Thornhill looks desperately towards the exit door.

EXT. HOUSE – DOLLY SHOT

Eve, Vandamm and Leonard have emerged from the house and are walking away from it towards the landing strip. Vandamm is holding Eve's arm. Leonard is walking behind them. They look off as they see:

REVERSE ANGLE: MOVING POINT OF VIEW
A twin-engined plane is letting down at the far end of the lighted runway, its landing lights ablaze.

EVE, VANDAMM AND LEONARD – DOLLY SHOT
The group are continuing their walk towards the plane. Now camera moves in to a close shot of Eve, as she walks. We see her anxious expression. The camera eases away to a three shot, and Eve's expression changes to a simulated nonchalant one.

CLOSE-UP: EVE
She looks over her shoulder, back towards the house.

POINT OF VIEW: THE HOUSE
No sign of Thornhill.

THREE SHOT
Vandamm is looking at Eve as she turns forward again.

> VANDAMM
> What is it?

> EVE
> *(vaguely)*
> I was wondering about those earrings . . .

> VANDAMM
> They'll turn up.

Camera eases in close on Eve again as she continues to walk. On her face we see increasing apprehension. She looks ahead.

POINT OF VIEW
The landed plane is taxiing towards the group. The silhouetted figure of Valerian is seen standing beside the baggage at the end of the runway.

ANOTHER ANGLE
The plane comes to a stop; the group arrives, and the cabin door is immediately opened from the inside. As Valerian starts to pass the baggage up to the man inside –

> CUT TO:

CLOSE-UP: EVE
She looks back towards the house with desperation.

POINT OF VIEW: THE HOUSE
Still no sign of Thornhill.

AT THE PLANE
While Valerian continues to dispose of the luggage, Vandamm, still holding Eve by the arm, turns to Leonard.

> VANDAMM
>
> When you return to New York, do say goodbye to my sister for me, and thank her for her superb performance as Mrs Townsend . . .

> LEONARD
>
> I'll do that.

> VANDAMM
> (*gesturing towards Valerian*)
>
> . . . And you might tell your knife-throwing chum that I've reassured his wife.

> LEONARD
>
> Right.

During this, Eve has been glancing about as though looking for a final means of escape. Her glance goes to Vandamm's hand still gripping her arm. She tries unsuccessfully to ease away from his grip. Leonard, seeing her actions, eases himself over to block any attempted escape she might be planning

> VANDAMM
>
> I guess that's all, Leonard.

He starts to lead Eve towards the steps of the plane.

> LEONARD
> (*looking at Eve*)
>
> Happy landing.

CLOSE-UP: EVE
Panic begins to seize her. Suddenly, from the house, comes the sound of two quick gunshots.

THE GROUP
All turn their heads quickly.

POINT OF VIEW: FLASH
*The flying figure of Thornhill is seen dashing out of the house and into
the sedan parked outside.*

THE GROUP
*Still looking off. Suddenly Eve, finding herself momentarily free of
Vandamm's grip and Leonard's observation, grabs the Tarascan
warrior from Vandamm's arm and dashes out of the scene towards the
house. Over this, we hear the distant car starting up. Leonard looks
quickly at Vandamm for instructions.*

VANDAMM
(sharply)

Get that figure back!

Leonard dashes away, with Valerian joining him.

REVERSE ANGLE
*Eve is running a few paces ahead of the two men, the sedan speeding
towards her. The car starts to pull up and its side door flies open as Eve
reaches it.*

SIDE-ON ANGLE
The car stops. Eve leaps in.

THORNHILL
(yells)

Lock it!

*She slams the door just as the two men arrive. They tug at the handle.
Thornhill guns the car away.*

MEDIUM SHOT
*The two men are flung back as the car drives off. It makes a wide circle
and speeds towards the house over rough ground.*

INT. CAR

                    EVE
                (*breathlessly*)
What happened? Are you all right?

                    THORNHILL
Can you imagine? The housekeeper had me pinned down for
five minutes before I realized it was that same silly gun of
yours.

He flashes a glance at the figure in her hands.

I see you got the . . . uh . . . pumpkin.

                    EVE
                (*grimly*)
Yes.

LANDING FIELD
Vandamm has just reached the two men.

                    VALERIAN
Don't worry, sir. The gates are locked.

AT THE GATES
*The car comes to a screeching stop before the locked gates. Thornhill
jumps out and starts tugging at the chains.*

CLOSE-UP: EVE IN CAR
*Still clutching the figure, she looks forward towards Thornhill anxiously,
then looks back.*

POINT OF VIEW
*With the house in the distance, she sees the running figures of Leonard
and Valerian.*

OBJECTIVE SHOT – THE CAR AND THE GATES
*Eve scrambles out of the car, runs towards Thornhill. He turns, sees the
men coming. Together, he and Eve run out of the shot.*

LEONARD AND VALERIAN
Running after them.

INT. FOREST. DOLLY SHOT – MOONLIGHT

The 'forest' is really no more than a shallow, heavily wooded area. Thornhill and Eve come running in, and camera moves with them as they scramble over rocks, fallen trees and other obstacles. Eve is encumbered by her scarf, handbag and the figure she is carrying.

THORNHILL

Here. Give me that.

He takes the figure from her. They run on. Suddenly Eve is brought up short as the scarf around her neck gets caught on a pine tree. Thornhill stops, turns to her and they struggle to get her loose.

FLASH: LEONARD AND VALERIAN
Crashing through the forest after them.

THORNHILL AND EVE
Still trying to extricate her. Finally they unwind her from the scarf, abandon it and run out of shot.

LEONARD AND VALERIAN
Running after them.

LONG SHOT: EXTERIOR FOREST
In the distance, we see the running figures of Thornhill and Eve emerge from the forest into an open clearing. They continue towards camera until, in a close shot, they come to a sudden stop and look off ahead.

POINT OF VIEW
About fifty to a hundred yards ahead, they see the back of the Mt Rushmore monument. The heads of the presidents are moonlit. Beyond is yawning space, and beyond that, the distant horizon.

THORNHILL'S VOICE

Uh oh. Didn't know you were here, gentlemen.

186

STRAIGHT ON TWO SHOT: THORNHILL AND EVE

THORNHILL
(*still looking ahead*)
No good this way. We're on top of the monument.

He now looks off to his right and slightly behind him.

POINT OF VIEW
In the distance, Valerian is seen emerging from the forest.

CLOSE SHOT: THORNHILL AND EVE
Eve, looking off in another direction, grabs Thornhill's arm.

EVE
Look!

Thornhill looks off.

POINT OF VIEW
Leonard has emerged from the woods in another spot.

PROFILE SHOT: THORNHILL AND EVE
He grabs her arm and starts running with her in the only direction they can go – towards the edge of the monument. Camera dollies along with them until they start slowing down. Camera comes to a stop.

REVERSE ANGLE: FULL VIEW OF PART OF MONUMENT
We see the tiny figures of Thornhill and Eve approach the edge.

WAIST SHOT: THORNHILL AND EVE
As they peer down.

POINT OF VIEW
The presidents' faces as seen from the edge, with moonlight revealing the depth below.

WAIST SHOT: THORNHILL AND EVE
They turn, look back once more at their pursuers.

THORNHILL

C'mon. Down we go.

EVE
(*looking down again*)

We can't.

THORNHILL

No choice. C'mon.

They start down and go out of shot.

LONG SHOT: CROSS ANGLE – THE MONUMENT
Shooting past Lincoln's face in foreground, we see Thornhill and Eve making their precarious way down the sloping crevice between Jefferson's face and the rear of Washington's head.

CLOSE ANGLE: THORNHILL AND EVE
As they work their way down:

THORNHILL
(*grimly*)

A funny thing happened to me the other day on my way to the theatre.

EVE

What?

THORNHILL

Skip it.

COMPREHENSIVE SHOT OF LEONARD AND VALERIAN
Still fairly far apart, arriving at the edge. Leonard is at the top of the crevice. Valerian is on Washington's head.

CLOSE ANGLE: THORNHILL AND EVE
They look up and see:

POINT OF VIEW
Leonard starting down after them.

MEDIUM SHOT: THORNHILL AND EVE
Continuing their perilous descent down the slope.

> THORNHILL

If we get out of this alive, let's go back to New York on a train together. All right?

> EVE

Is that a proposition?

> THORNHILL

No – a proposal.

He loses his footing, slips, dangles precariously. Eve reaches down, tries to help him.

> EVE

What happened to the first two marriages?

> THORNHILL
> *(struggling)*

My wives divorced me.

> EVE

Why?

> THORNHILL
> *(still struggling)*

I think they , . . said I . . . led . . . too dull a life . . .

He regains a safe foothold.

CLOSE SHOT: VALERIAN
Sliding rapidly down a sloping ledge to Washington's right shoulder and starting across.

LONG SHOT: CROSS ANGLE – THE MONUMENT
With Lincoln's nose and lips in foreground, we see Valerian making his way across beneath Washington's chin to head off Thornhill and Eve, who are coming down towards Washington's left shoulder with Leonard scrambling down after them.

HIGH ANGLE: LEONARD
Below him in background are Thornhill and Eve. Leonard accidentally dislodges a precariously balanced rock. It starts to tumble down the slope.

CLOSE SHOT: THORNHILL AND EVE
Their backs are to camera. They hear the rumbling rock, turn, eyes wide with dismay. There is no time for them to move out of the path of disaster.

POINT OF VIEW
The rock is crashing down towards camera. At the last moment, just as it is about to smash into its intended victims, the rock hits a snag and goes flying off at a tangent into the yawning depths below.

THORNHILL AND EVE
For a brief moment, stunned into immobility by their brush with death.

> EVE
> (*in a hollow voice*)
> I just thought of a new drink . . .

> THORNHILL
> (*still staring ahead*)
> Really?

> EVE
> People, on-the-rocks.

Thornhill gives her a look. She gives a little shrug. And then they quickly start down the ledge on Washington's left shoulder. (Right here, Eve's handbag, shoes and suit jacket become hopelessly encumbering. Thornhill makes her get rid of whatever she can. The shoes go flying away. So, too, the jacket, with womanly regrets. But Eve makes Thornhill stuff some of the contents of her handbag into his pockets before she hurls the handbag to the depths below. During this striptease, there should be some ad-libbed comments.) Preoccupied with their physical efforts, they are not aware of Valerian approaching in background. *He gets closer and closer and now, with upraised knife, is about to stab Thornhill when Eve, turning suddenly, sees Valerian and shouts:*

Look out!

Thornhill swings around, hits Valerian's wrist and deflects the downward arc of the knife in mid-air. Then he quickly gives Eve the figure, *and shouts:*

THORNHILL

Keep going . . . !

Eve moves on, with Leonard coming down after her, as Thornhill faces Valerian again.

CLOSE ANGLE: THORNHILL AND VALERIAN
Struggling to the death, with the knife poised between them in Valerian's hand.

THORNHILL
(*gasping*)
I'm beginning . . . to think . . . you don't . . . *like* me . . .

They wrestle each other to the ground, then roll over the edge and begin to slide down towards a precipitous drop, still struggling.

CLOSE SHOT: EVE
*Looking back for a moment just as the two men start their slide. She
turns away and scrambles on as she sees Leonard almost upon her.*

THORNHILL AND VALERIAN
*Still sliding down. At the very edge of the precipice, Thornhill manages
to break free, and* the sudden release causes Valerian to plunge to
his death with a terrible scream. *Thornhill gets to his feet, looks off,
sees Leonard about to catch up with Eve. He starts towards them.*

CLOSE ANGLE: EVE AND LEONARD
*Leonard grabs Eve, wrests the figure from her grasp and gives her a
vicious shove that sends her down to what appears to be certain death.
But as she slips down, she manages to catch hold of a ridge in the
precipitous slope and dangles there, unable to move.*

ANOTHER ANGLE
*As Thornhill arrives on the scene, Leonard is starting away with the
figure. Thornhill clambers down to rescue Eve.*

THORNHILL

Hang on!

*He lowers himself down to Eve, placing himself in a perilous position.
His only purchase is one hand gripping the edge above him while the
other hand reaches out to take Eve's outstretched hand.*

CLOSE SHOT: EVE
*In her effort to reach Thornhill's hand, her feet apply pressure to the
ridge she has been standing on. Just as their hands meet, the ridge
breaks off and her legs dangle in mid-air.*

OBJECTIVE SHOT
*Thornhill, hanging on to the ledge above him with one hand, is holding
Eve from death below with his other hand.*

CLOSE SHOT: THORNHILL
*Turning into camera with desperation to look over the ledge above him.
He sees:*

POINT OF VIEW
Leonard still moving away.

CLOSE SHOT: THORNHILL

THORNHILL

Leonard!

POINT OF VIEW: FROM THORNHILL
Leonard stops, turns and looks back.

THORNHILL'S VOICE
(*off-screen*)

For God's sake . . .

Leonard starts down towards him. As he approaches, the camera begins to pan down his body until suddenly Thornhill's hand appears in foreground gripping the ledge. The feet of Leonard slowly approach and come to a stop a few inches from the hand. Then one foot is raised and gently placed on the hand.

CLOSE-UP: THORNHILL
Glancing up sharply, reacting as he feels the pressure of the shoe on his fingers and realizes what is about to happen.

CLOSE-UP: LEONARD
Looking down without expression as he leans forward slightly and deliberately applies the full weight of his body on to the fingers.

CLOSE-UP: THORNHILL
In horrible agony.

THORNHILL
(*gasps*)

Don't . . . I . . . can't . . .

Eve cries out.

CLOSE-UP – SHOE PRESSED ON HAND

> THORNHILL'S VOICE
> (*off-screen*)
> Have to . . . let . . . *go* . . .

Suddenly there is the crack of a gun which reverberates through the monument. The shoe relaxes its pressure for a moment and the figure drops from Leonard's grasp to the ledge beside the hand and smashes, revealing several rolls of microfilm.

LONG SHOT: TOP OF THE MONUMENT
A brief flash of a group of silhouetted figures looking down.

CLOSE-UP: THORNHILL
Glancing briefly at the smashed figure and the microfilm, then looking up.

LOW ANGLE: LEONARD
Mortally wounded, looking down with dying eyes, then starting to fall towards camera.

THORNHILL AND EVE
Recoiling as Leonard's body falls past them.

LOW ANGLE: TOP OF MONUMENT
In a full figure shot, we see the group on the monument at close range: the Professor, holding a pair of binoculars; Vandamm, flanked by two uniformed State Troopers, one of whom is holding the revolver that fired the shot. Below them, two more State Police clamber down the slope to rescue Thornhill and Eve and disappear out of shot.

> PROFESSOR
> (*staring down worriedly*)
> Well done, Sergeant.

> VANDAMM
> (*sardonically*)
> Rather unsporting, don't you think . . . using real bullets?

CUT TO:

BIG HEAD CLOSE-UP: THORNHILL
Looking down with tension on his face.

> THORNHILL
> *(with exertion)*

Here . . . reach . . . *now* . . .

> EVE'S VOICE
> *(off-screen – gasping)*

I'm . . . trying . . .

> THORNHILL

Come on . . . I've got you . . . *up* . . .

BIG HEAD CLOSE-UP: EVE
Looking up, her face showing physical effort.

> EVE

Can't make it –

> THORNHILL'S VOICE
> *(off-screen)*

Yes you can . . . Come on . . .

> EVE
> *(strained)*

Pull harder . . .

BIG HEAD CLOSE-UP: THORNHILL.

> THORNHILL

There . . . that's it . . .

BIG HEAD CLOSE-UP: EVE

> EVE
> *(moving up)*

Ah . . . good . . .

She starts to laugh.

MEDIUM SHOT: THORNHILL AND EVE
As she lands beside him, we realize that they are not on Mt Rushmore after all, but are sitting side by side, feet dangling from the upper berth of

*a drawing-room in a train standing in a station at night. He has been
lifting her up with difficulty because the lower berth is not open. From
outside, a voice calls out: 'Board!'*

                              EVE
                       (*still laughing*)
        This is silly, Thornhill.

                          THORNHILL
        I know. But I'm sentimental.

*He puts his arms around her, and as they kiss lovingly, we see the hand
that was stepped on.* Each finger is neatly taped with a Band-Aid.
Just then, the train jerks into motion.

EXT. TRAIN

*We are shooting towards the rear of the observation car as the train rolls
off into the night.*

        FADE OUT:

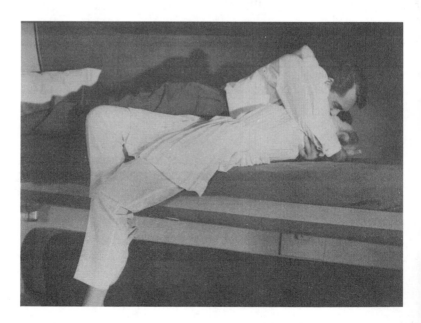